Two Shall Be One

Two Shall Be One

RUTH HARMS CALKIN

David C. Cook Publishing Co.

ELGIN, ILLINOIS   WESTON, ONTARIO   LA HABRA, CALIFORNIA

© 1977 David C. Cook Publishing Co.
Published by David C. Cook Publishing Co.
850 N. Grove Ave., Elgin, IL 60120.
Printed in the United States of America.

Library of Congress Catalog Number 76-23349
ISBN 0-89191-057-3

Photo credits:
Ray Atkeson/Devaney, p. 14
Alon Reininger/de Wys, p. 18
Leo de Wys, Inc., pp. 22, 78, 88, 96
Jay Hoops/de Wys, p. 34
Orville Andrews, p. 40
Fred Baldwin/de Wys, p. 46
H. Armstrong Roberts, pp. 52, 74, 78, 122

DEDICATION

You . . .
Hold my heart in yours
As gently as a rose holds a dewdrop
As quietly as the sky holds a star.

You . . .
Hold my heart in yours
As majestically as a mountain holds a pine
As harmoniously as a song holds a melody.

You . . .
Hold my heart in yours
As faithfully as a prayer holds an answer
As lovingly as my heart holds yours.

You . . .
My husband
I love being married to you.

CONTENTS

Though It Takes a Lifetime

Lord—
Sometimes I wonder
How two imperfect people
Can possibly build
A perfect marriage.
And then I stop wondering
For I know they cannot.

But this they can do:
They can invite You
The perfect One
To share day by day
In their togetherness.
Gently, carefully
You will nurture them.
You will transform
Their imperfections.

Though it takes a lifetime
Their marriage will bear
Luscious fruit . . . like a tree
Planted along a river bank—
And all that they do
Shall prosper.

How the Letters Began

Only a few sentences in Julie's letter ended with ordinary periods. Exclamation points splashed over the pages flamboyantly. I knew her delicious joy had personally dictated each one. What else can you do when you're exploding with love, and you simply have to tell somebody about it?

Dear Ruth,
I have the most wonderful news! I'm in love, and his name is Kent! Suddenly I know that nothing in my life will ever be the same again! You'll like him, I just know you will! I can hardly wait for you to meet him!

He's a man—a real man—and he treats me like a woman, not like a helpless little child. I don't have to pretend to him or try to be somebody I'm not. Kent wants me to be me, just me, and we can be honest and open with each other! I can be *me* best when I'm with him!

We talk about everything. Little things . . . big things . . . music . . . books . . . ideas . . . our dreams and goals . . . just everything. I've never talked to anybody very much before, and Kent always understands. I feel comfortable and—well, just *complete*—when we're together.

It's hard to believe this is happening to me. Even ordinary things are exciting now—like eating popcorn, or walking in pouring rain, or listening to crickets . . . things like that.

Once I told Kent I thought I had swallowed liquid sunshine! He just laughed (his laugh sort of rings) and he said, "It's bound to rain someday. But don't worry—I'll be your umbrella."

I'm sure God brought us together. Kent's love for God is deep and beautiful. He doesn't talk about it a lot, but when he does, it's real. We both want our marriage to honor God!

Did you notice? I said *marriage!* Are you surprised? We're going to be married next summer, soon after graduation. We can hardly wait. . . .

The letter went on, page after page, then finally the question on page 6:

May I come to visit you during the semester break? Kent will be working, but I'll be home for a few days. I just have to tell you all about him!

Love,
Julie

I couldn't help but smile. After six long pages of small, cramped script, I rather assumed the subject of "him" had been amply covered. I was very wrong.

So three weeks later, we sat at the counter in my yellow kitchen, just the two of us, eating cookies and drinking hot tea.

It was fun being together again—laughing, sharing, just as we'd done before. Julie had been one of our "children" since she was a piano student of mine back in grade-school days, and our kitchen counter had often been the scene for our jumbled conversations.

12

For at least two hours that afternoon, I listened to a love-filled account of a future husband named Kent—everything about him from his hairstyle (just perfect) to his ardent love for surfing. There never seemed to be any subject break.

Then suddenly she said, "Ruth, you've been married—well, practically *forever!* But look at me—I have so much to learn about marriage. More than anything, I want to be a super-good wife, but it all seems so big!"

How beautiful she looked at that moment! I touched her arm. "Julie, it *is* big. All God's plans are big. But the wonderful thing is—he's in them with us. We can always keep learning and growing because God shows us how. Not for a moment are we on our own."

"Would you be willing to share what you've learned?" she asked pensively.

And so the letters began. Surprisingly, they continued for many months.

Letters about living and learning and loving . . . letters about laughter and tears . . . about trusting and praying . . . about sharing and listening and forgiving . . . about growing and knowing.

Letters about the rich and beautiful things God longs to do for a bride and groom—in fact, for *any* married couple—when he is invited to live in their home, in their marriage, *in their lives.*

Letters about marriage!

If I Could Have My Wish...

Dear Julie,
You should see the notes cluttering my desk! Corners of envelopes, a few registration cards, a paper napkin, even a small brown sack—all with hurriedly scribbled reminders of things I want to share with you.

The truth is—thoughts of you are no small thing around here. You've pushed and pulled at my heart ever since our last visit together. I shop for groceries, make the bed, dust furniture, and suddenly I picture you doing exactly the same things. You probably envision a lot more exciting things, but eventually you *will* have to dust!

Julie, even now I can scarcely believe it. To think that we actually sat in our kitchen, you and I, talking about your engagement and contemplated wedding! What in the world happened to the years . . . the days . . . the moments? Just yesterday, it seems, we were talking about your new puppy and roller skates and Christmas programs and piano lessons.

Julie, I'll be writing frequently as I promised, but today I'm going to share some letters from four collegians—all friends of ours. The letters express some practical Christian concepts relating to marriage.

Dear Ruth,

I've thought a lot about our conversation regarding marriage. What kind of a wife would I like to be? Well, first I want to be a truly godly woman, one who loves God with everything she has and is. He must come before anyone else. I want my husband to know he's loved and supported. I hope I can always be a joy and comfort to him. I want to be a woman who laughs easily, who forgives easily, and who listens well.

I'd like to be a fairly efficient housekeeper, but just enough to make the house a home. I think a husband should enjoy his home. I want to let my husband know he's the greatest man in the world—especially when he doesn't *feel* like he is.

I'd like to be a great cook, but believe me, God is going to have to help me with this one. I can even burn water!

Wherever the Lord puts us, I pray I'll be able to make a home *seem* like a home—whether it's a lovely house on a hilltop or a grass hut in Africa!

Paula

Dear Ruth,

I really want the girl I marry to love Christ more than she loves me. I guess I want to be able to count on her to stand firm even in my weaknesses.

I hope we will both always feel each other's prayerful support. I pray there will be a co-sharing of God's endowments to us—the fulfillment of the uncompleted "half" in both of us.

I really want her to be "easy to look at"! But I want her beauty to come from her inner life.

Above all, I want both of us to trust Christ completely.

Dru

16

Dear Ruth,
Above all, I want the girl I marry to be a Christian. We must have things in common. She doesn't have to be cute if she has an outgoing personality. Both would be terrific! We must be able to communicate even about small things. A sharing marriage is a loving marriage.

Rick

Dear Ruth,
God is first in Jon's life. That's what first attracted me to him. His honesty and leadership qualities attracted me, too. He enjoys simple things like flying a kite or an afternoon drive. He shows me I'm special in a thousand ways.

Gail

Julie, what these collegians are basically saying is this: Jesus Christ is the Master Architect and Builder of homes. A Christian marriage is meant to be a joyful, dynamic relationship. But it must be linked to his power.

Years ago, while sitting under a sprawling oak tree on the University of Oregon campus, I wrote a letter to Rollie telling him the kind of wife I wanted to be. I haven't always lived up to those high and noble goals. I've failed a thousand times—God knows this, and so does Rollie. But I am loved, and the goals still glisten.

Right now you are living on a beautiful tree-lined campus. On a sunny day, why don't you grab a pencil, find your own sprawling tree, and write a letter!

Wedding Prayer

Dear Julie,
One day, after one of our serious talks, I shared a prayer with you written by a bride on the morning of her wedding day. With a burst of enthusiasm (so typically you) you asked for a copy. I share it with you gladly . . . .

Dear Lord,
It's really here—our wedding day! Just six hours from now, in a hushed and beautiful sanctuary, we'll be kneeling at the altar to give our lives to each other . . . forever!

Lord, we couldn't have asked for a more beautiful day. You've made it vibrant with music and laughter . . . all glistening and sun-streaked. Thank you so much!

Thank you for guiding us, a day at a time, through all the hectic hours of planning and arranging . . . for keeping us (in most instances) reasonably frenzy-free. There *were* a few rough spots, Lord. Quite a few! (Mostly my fault.) I can see that I have a lot to learn. I'm really counting on your help.

Thank you for all the ridiculous little things—jokes and quips—which cleared the atmosphere when petty annoyances drifted in.

Another very special thanks, Lord, for miraculously (and I do mean miraculously) helping us to stay within our limited budget, despite my sudden heart-flips over all those *outrageous* prices. You even stretched the dollars by giving us enough good sense to whittle down our want-list.

Thank you for my bridal showers and for all our lovely wedding gifts. Most of them were chosen so personally. Now, please show me how to be gracious and explicit in my thank-you notes. And help me to write quickly, Lord. You know what a problem I always have with letters.

Lord, thank you for loving, patient parents who really supported us all the way, and for family and friends who have run a thousand errands without a breath of complaint.

God, as I talk to you just now, my joy is almost more than I can contain. You are giving us a rare and priceless gift—*the gift of each other*—to cherish forever.

I'm happy. I'm excited. But I'm frightened, too. What a thunderous declaration you've given in your Word: "The two shall become one flesh." Though we understand the words but vaguely now, teach us their full significance as we live and love together.

Tonight, for the very first time, we shall belong to each other completely. *For the very first time.* I say these five words with gratitude and freedom. It was your love, Lord, your special power, that held us to our mutual resolve.

There were moments of fierce temptation. God, you know! The months of waiting seemed endless for a love as eager as ours. There were moments of tension. Moments of sweeping desire. Some of our friends bombarded us with persuasive arguments. One or two ridiculed when we attempted to explain your biblical concept.

But with growing devotion to each other, with renewed dedication to your sacred plan, we determined to recite our marriage vows free from tarnished memories . . . from smudges of guilt . . . from fear and regret.

Always, Lord, I'll cherish the stumbling words of my dearest love one fragrant moonlit night:

"I love you so much that with all my *heart* I want you . . . and I love you so much that with all my *will* I won't."

That night, Lord, I knew with beautiful assurance that he was your man *first*—even before he was my man.

It was easier after that. Much easier.

Tonight at our elegant hotel, in the quiet privacy of our own room, there will be sudden new discoveries . . . and more discoveries. There will be an intimacy surpassing anything we've ever known.

Undoubtedly there will be some tense, awkward moments. After all, we're just beginning a lifelong venture. Lord, keep us both tender and understanding, always eager to please, to give, to receive, always eager to bring delight to each other.

The very first time! Thank you, Lord, for punctuating our promise to wait with your power to obey. May our waiting *before* our wedding keep the wanting going strong *after* our wedding.

Tonight we'll close our door to all the world. But not to you, Lord. I trust never to you. Where you are, there is always joy.

And, Lord, in our marriage we do anticipate joy!

A Promise Is for Keeping

Dear Julie,

I'm sitting at the round maple table in our dining room. Two crazy little birds are singing their hearts out on our front lawn, each trying absurdly to outsing the other. Their chirping adds a melodic descant to my clicking typewriter.

The password this morning is joy! Joy laughing and singing and chasing sunbeams all over the hills. There's something nostalgic in the atmosphere, something exciting. I don't know what, exactly. The subtle fragrances, perhaps—or the warm September sun. Maybe it's the blazing panorama of color: orange, scarlet, gold, wherever you look.

Or maybe it's just that today happens to be the third of September—our wedding anniversary!

Can you believe it, Julie? Thirty years. What a lot of living two people can stuff into thirty giant-sized years. What a lot of sharing and caring and laughing and crying. What a lot of love—*what an immense amount of love.*

The other day a friend asked, "Knowing what you know now about marriage, the good and the bad of it, the ups and downs, would you do it all over again?"

I couldn't help but smile. My eager response was, "If I could marry the same husband—yes. I'd start tomorrow. No, I'd start today!"

This morning at the front door, after a hard male kiss, Rollie grabbed me and said, "I love being committed to you!" I probably looked startled. I don't remember that he's ever said it quite like that before. Usually he says, "I love being married to you," but this was different. I've been thinking about it all day: *I love being committed to you . . .*

A commitment, Julie, is a vow, a pledge, a *promise*—and our attitude toward commitment has a very vital bearing on our attitude toward marriage.

When I was little, it was my mother who first taught me the intrinsic value of a promise. Mother was an exceptional teacher. Her lessons were always taught in the most impressive way—by personal example.

We learned very early in our family that mother's integrity was unblemished—so whenever we wanted to go somewhere, or do something special, we knew exactly when our wish would be granted: the moment we could persuade her to say "I promise."

Words like "maybe" or "perhaps" or "We'll see" were wobbly words. The decision could go either way. But a promise was as sure as sunshine, as certain as six o'clock. It never occurred to us to remind mother of a promise or to ask again. We knew—we always *knew*—we'd go to the circus, or we'd stay overnight with a friend, or we'd pop popcorn after dinner, or whatever. Once having committed herself, that was it. A promise was a promise, made solemnly in good faith, and carried out despite weariness, inconvenience, or personal sacrifice.

Mother was eager to instill her conviction in us! Her emphatic words still brush against my memory: "Never say 'I promise' unless you really intend to keep your word." Then, with a twinkle in her blue-gray eyes, she would add, "Remember, a promise is for keeping!" Her oft-repeated words left a permanent imprint on my life. I began to learn at an early age something of the meaning of commitment.

Hundreds of times in our marriage Rollie and I have made promises. The word *commitment* is as much a part of us as the furniture in our home. No, much more. The furniture could be demolished tomorrow.

But thirty years ago, before God and to each other, we made a life-commitment. "As long as forever is"—that was our vow—our settled decision. We didn't slide into it, nor did we crawl or drift into it. There was nothing casual or careless about it. With our minds, our wills, and our hearts wide-open, we pledged. Willingly and openly we assumed a personal responsibility. We were accountable to each other.

Our commitment involves our investment of time and talent and energy. It means vulnerability. It involves our moods, our risks, our personal choices—our dreams and disappointments.

It involves our love, rich and abiding, bigger by far than we had ever dreamed. Where there is genuine love, there is freedom. Freedom to express, to respond, to listen, to learn. Love eliminates completely a grin-and-bear-it acceptance. Commitment is love doing, love giving, love in action with never a thought of quitting.

It is a serious thing to make a commitment to someone else. It puts enormous demands on us. It tests our patience, our integrity, our vitality. It tests our ability to adjust—to accept each other without reservation. Marriage deals with real problems, with real decisions, with real conflicts, but so does all of life!

Granted, we take a few tumbles along the way. We stub our toes and skin our knees from time to time. But nobody with an ounce of grit ever stops in the middle of a venture because of a skinned knee.

My friend Mark said one day, "Doesn't a commitment bind you? Don't you feel chained by it?" On the contrary, a commitment frees us to explore, to climb, to keep our eyes on the goal. All enticing detours simply lead to dead ends. We may do some heavy trudging, but that's when we depend upon each other most. Out of desperation comes aspiration.

Julie, I believe our love continues to grow because our commitment to each other is superseded by another commitment: our personal commitment to God. You see, years ago we discovered that we simply could not be God to each other. It is utterly impossible for any couple to find in each other what can be found in God alone. How insecure we would be if our dependency centered on anyone or anything that we could lose.

But God is our security—God, who can never be lost! In every marriage it is the greater commitment to God that makes the lesser commitment to each other as shining as silver and as durable as gold.

The thing that makes it so stupendous is this: The One to whom we are committed is eternally committed to us. We have his assured word for it: "In everything you do, put God first, and he will direct you and crown your efforts with success" (Proverbs 3:6, Living Bible).

I trust you and Kent will always remember: *A promise is for keeping.*

From My Journal
Commitment means we take the
very worst of each other, the very
best of each other, and the
in-between of each other; then,
stirring it all together, we say with
gentle understanding, "I love and
totally accept the mixture of you."

Take Me to My Leader

Dear Julie,
Your letter is here on my desk—the letter in which you asked directly, "Do you consider yourself a *submissive* wife?" You may not remember, but you underscored the word *submissive* with a bold stroke of your pen.

Did it occur to you that you might be asking the wrong person? I have a feeling Rollie would be your most reliable resource. Believe me, he could come up with some fascinating details after thirty years of living with me.

But I want to tell you my honest conviction about a very stalwart biblical principle. I am personally persuaded, on the basis of the Bible, that submission is an *attitude*—the recognition of masculine leadership in marriage. It is my willingness to accept the authority God has entrusted to my husband. It is indeed a trust.

Through the years I have learned, and I'm still learning, that when I submit to my husband's dynamic leadership in areas for which God holds him directly responsible, the path is amazingly smooth. Our relationship is restful and satisfying, and my sense of fulfillment is at high peak. I am not incessantly trying to prove something to myself or anyone else. I can live with myself contentedly. I have a sound basis for praying, "God, I don't ask you to take sides. Just take over." With beautiful dexterity, he does.

The fifth chapter of Ephesians clearly states: "Wives, submit yourselves unto your own husbands, as unto the Lord."

There it stands, stable and workable. God never apologizes for a decision. He never "corrects" a directive. But invariably he teaches us, with infinite patience and skill, that obedience always brings his intended blessing—*always*, Julie.

The verse in no way suggests that I am inferior. It simply indicates that we do indeed function differently. If we are to avoid confusion and chaos, there cannot be two leaders. As the saying goes, "In a council of two, there can be no majority." It is my understanding that God has made my husband responsible for making final decisions.

Frankly, there have been very few times in our marriage when decision-making has involved a major conflict. Usually we are able to come to an agreement without a catastrophic bounce-around. I remember a time when we were totally divided on an issue. I had sufficient wisdom to *say* little and *pray* much. However, my talk with God was certainly slanted toward *my* opinion: "Lord, I think Rollie is completely mistaken. Please talk to him. Whatever it takes, help him to change his mind. You know how determined he is, so you'd better work fast!"

I was writing my prayer that morning (as I so often do), and right at the end of the sentence there came the convicting thought, "Don't ask me to make your husband what *you* want him to be. Just ask me to make him what *I* want him to be."

What do you do with an admonition like that? Well, if you've had previous experience (and I have), you *obey* it.

As it happened, Rollie was right. But he isn't always. Decision-making involves risk. No husband is infallible. No wife is infallible. There may be errors in judgment, an occasional wrong choice. At times a wrong choice may incur drastic complications. At such times it is imperative that we encourage and support each other. A bitter "I told you so" in no way corrects the damage. It only builds a wall of isolation.

Our observation has been that God is able to make even a wrong choice contribute to our highest good when our motivation is sincere and when our loyalty to each other is intact.

Does the principle of submission devalue my potential? Not at all. Do I make decisions? Certainly. Without always running to my husband? Of course. Does he trust me? In some areas, more than he trusts himself!

I am certainly not thwarted or confined. I am not pushed aside like an ornament after Christmas. My capabilities are not shelved. I do not feel threatened. I don't chirp, flutter, or play coy little games to prove my "submissiveness." I am a woman—with a legitimate right to my individuality. How is all this possible? Well, Paul goes on to say: "For the husband is the head of the wife, even as Christ is the head of the church. . . . Husbands, love your wives, even as Christ also loved the church, and gave himself for it. . . ."

I have a profound appreciation for the two little words *even as*. They forcefully indicate that a husband is to exert his leadership with all the genuine love and compassion of Jesus Christ. What enormous implications! Think about it, Julie—*could any wife ask for more?*

Can you imagine a wife feeling stifled or restricted if her husband has one growing desire—to be subject to Christ, as

Christ is subject to the will of his Father?

Would it be a repulsive thought, a terrifying ordeal, to submit to a husband who reflected the lavish love that Christ demonstrated for his church?

Would any wife feel she was "submerging her dreams" by submitting to a love that is abundantly kind and forgiving . . . a love that refuses to maneuver or manipulate or coerce . . . a love that embraces faults and lays everything on the line in sacrificial giving?

I remember how I used to stand on a tall kitchen stool when I was little, my chubby arms extended, just waiting for my father to say, "All right, honey—now jump!"

For a split second I'd hesitate, then I'd laughingly throw myself into dad's strong, sheltering arms. It was great fun. I always begged to do it again. You see, I *trusted*.

Loving Kent as you do, can you trust his integrity and honesty? Can you trust him to assume responsibility for you? To protect you and plan for you? Can you trust him to make decisions based on his loyal concern? Your *trust*, Julie, is another word for submission.

I'll never forget Rollie's prayer one morning at the breakfast table: "Lord, make me the husband you want me to be—first for your sake; then for Ruth's sake."

We were having waffles for breakfast, and as I poured the syrup, I felt my heart pouring out as well. I could trust a husband who prayed like that.

Ephesians 5 is literally loaded with gold nuggets. Here's still another: "Honor Christ by submitting to each other." In other words, Paul is letting us know that submission is not a muddy one-way street for wives only. The husband is not the undisputed czar in his home, who makes arbitrary decisions without an ounce of concern for his wife. A wife need not stifle her intellect or repress her ideas for fear of deflating her husband's masculinity.

I know what you're thinking. I can feel the vibrations all the way from your campus to my kitchen. Thoughts like: *Wonderful! Beautiful! I'm all for it! But where in all the world is there a husband who reflects the unconditional love of Christ all the time? Where is there a wife who joyfully submits, never tangling or wrangling with her own emotional conflicts? I mean—after all . . .*

Yes, Julie, I know I've described the ideal. We don't always succeed every hour of every day. We're vulnerable, susceptible, moody, and too often contentious.

Nevertheless, there is the goal. Or rather, Christ is the goal!

It is his love in our lives, in our marriage, that makes the tremendous difference. When we put no limits on him, he shows us the way. Then he enables us to *act* on what he reveals.

The shimmering secret is this: *The more totally we both submit to Jesus Christ, the more joyfully we will submit to each other!*

I believed this, Julie, the first year we were married—but with a few ominous clouds hovering over my independent spirit. Today I believe it with unwavering conviction. It works—as God said it would.

In my next letter I want to tell you how I learned in a drastic, painful way to submit to my husband's spiritual leadership. It happened a long time ago, but the memory is vivid. Don't be alarmed—it all turned out beautifully!

He Can Match Every Dream

Dear Julie,

I'm having a turbulent struggle with myself today. I promised to share my personal battle of long ago, but as I begin to put it down, black print on white paper, I'm suddenly aware that you will have a grim and glaring revelation of me. But here goes . . .

Before we were married, the thing that jolted me with joy was Rollie's major at the University of Oregon. He was up to his neck in commercial art, and I liked everything about it. I had more lavish dreams for our bright future than anybody could stuff into one soaring heart.

Often we'd go to the campus together, and I'd sit for hours on a tall wooden stool, pensively watching as flaming colors splashed over the canvas. Frequently I'd envision the home we'd have—a home of elegant style and charm. I was sure commercial artists earned enormous salaries, and my husband was bound to be good.

It wasn't that I'd minded our old-fashioned parsonages with their high ceilings and heavy sliding doors and walk-in pantries. Even as I write to you, I remember friendly kitchens and cobwebby attics and damp basements (cellars, we called them) with row after row of canned fruits and vegetables.

But it was different now. I wanted to see the world from the other side. To see it with Rollie was my fondest dream.

Our wedding was beautiful, and after a glorious five-day honeymoon we began to give our small, unsuspecting apartment a radical face-lift. We attempted things we'd never tried before. Our spirits were full of adventure, and every new innovation seemed to call for another.

One day as we were slipcovering the couch, I said blissfully, "Oh, honey, before too long we'll be able to buy a new couch—our very own. Won't it be wonderful?"

Then it came pouncing—an unbelievably shattering day. It left me groping and grasping. I simply wasn't prepared for it.

It was about lunchtime, and Rollie came dashing through the front door of our apartment delirious with excitement. The shoulders of his heart seemed to touch the sky.

As I write to you now, Julie, I can still catch the vibrancy in Rollie's voice as he shouted the "good news." He had been invited to join the staff of the First Baptist Church of Eugene (our home church at that time) as minister of music and Christian education. Wasn't it miraculous? he wanted to know.

Frankly, no! In no way did this fit into my satin-lined box of personal dreams. I bluntly said so.

I knew that Rollie had often prayed for this opportunity, long before we were married. I knew too of the quiet morning he had utterly committed his life to God. Anything . . . anywhere . . . always . . . he had vowed. There had been no shaking, bulldozer changes—just the confident trust that God had heard—and smiled. Rollie continued his major, but always with the hopeful thought of something more. Was God now giving us a fleeting glimpse of the future? Undoubtedly my husband thought so.

I just stood there, stoical and unresponding.

I finally managed to come up with something dramatic and curt (I'd probably read it in some magazine): "So this is the way a girl's dream comes to an end—all in a moment, just like that." On the last word I snapped my fingers.

Rollie's response was less dramatic but far more effective. "Honey, we can't disregard God's direction. We both know that. He'll show us the way if we let him, and I'm willing for the change to be in me. But we *must* be together. Will you talk to him with me?"

The following morning I found a note on the breakfast table.

Darling . . . your happiness is more important to me than anything in the world. I'm willing to invest energy, time, money, everything in our marriage. I have pledged myself to take care of you always.

Sometimes, I suppose, I'll have to make decisions on my own, and I'll count on you to stand by me. Undoubtedly you will make some decisions on your own, and I'll stand by you. But *this* decision is one we absolutely must make together.

I've often told you of the strange urgency within me. I think it started the day I sat in your father's office and we talked for several hours. This was even before you and I were going together. Since then, I've never been free from wondering if God had something more for me—and now for us. That's why we must consider the invitation that has come.

However, this is to let you know I will not force the issue. It would never work. God will show us both. I will not give any answer until we come to a mutual agreement—however we decide. In the meantime, please know I love you with all of my being.

That day, although I wasn't conscious of it, God was launching an intensive training program in my life. He was determined to teach me the biblical principle of spiritual leadership in our home. If we were to gain new ground together, we simply could not be spiritually divided.

The next few weeks were miserable and lonely. I was like a whimpering orphan—hedged in, pushed about, bumping into concrete walls of my own selfishness.

Rollie was kind and gentle—and very, very careful with me. When we talked, he didn't press the issue or point out my obvious lack of submission. We both knew we couldn't go into the ministry with a halfway commitment. Rollie patiently waited for God's timing.

Often during the stretched-out weeks I couldn't help but think of the words my father had frequently quoted: "He that doeth the will of God abideth forever." Again and again I'd trip over them.

God seemed to be relentless. He kept hitting me where it hurt. Every song, every sermon, every word became a painful stab. I could hide the Bible under the bed or in a drawer, but I couldn't quiet the echo in my struggling heart.

Then one damp October day I finally faced God honestly and directly. I couldn't put him off any longer. To hinder his plan by my foolish rebellion was too great a risk. I could no more change God's principles or alter his commands than I could crush the Grand Canyon. I could, however, crush myself—if I persisted in my stubborn pride.

Before our wedding, we had invited Jesus Christ to live in our home forever. He had every right to be the Great First, and I knew it. *Surely he could match every dream of mine!*

At last the crisis ended. Rollie had undoubtedly done a lot

of private praying. Now I could tell him I wanted God's will for both of us. I could believe, or at least *begin* to believe, that biblical submission meant my joyful fulfillment. God was for us, not against us.

As we talked that day, intimately and tenderly, our happiness knew no bounds. We laughed, sang, teased, loved, prayed, and praised. Then we went out and bought the biggest hamburgers we could find anywhere in town!

Have we been disappointed? Has life cheated us? Have we missed out on the goodies? No, no! Not once have we regretted the decision. *Not once.*

God turned us around. He started us on a new path of continued service, and as we walked in the sunlight he pointed to diamonds.

Julie, that's what I envision for you and Kent. God has not called Kent into the ministry, but his profession is nevertheless sacred. God's place for us is always sacred—wherever it is. Kent needs your love and loyal support all the way.

God tells us that his mighty power at work within us is able to do far more than we could ever dare to ask or even dream—infinitely beyond our highest prayers, desires, thoughts, or hopes. Read it for yourself in the third chapter of Ephesians.

But in the process of "his work within us," he wants to teach you three things:

He won't let you go!
He won't let you off!
He wants you to win—in him!

It Isn't Always Spring

Dear Julie,
Remember the old story?

"And as they rode off into the sunset, the prince promised her his love, his riches, and his castle in the clouds, if only she would be his. She agreed. Later, after the wedding . . ."

It's going to happen one day—it's bound to. There's going to be an "after the wedding." I can't tell you when, exactly. Maybe on the tenth of April, maybe on the twelfth of June, maybe somewhere in between. Could be you'll miss the date completely, the way time flies and all.

But some weary evening after the honeymoon you'll flop down in your favorite chair, kick off your shoes, brush a strand of hair from your pretty face, and all of a sudden it will hit you:

The sky isn't etched with banners of gold. The air isn't lilac-sweet. You don't seem to be catching your breath between wild kisses all the time. No heart tremors. Butterflies seem to take naps. In marriage it isn't always spring!

Maybe on the fifth of March, maybe on the eighth of August, you'll pick up your wedding book with all its reminders of that happy event. And then, unexpectedly, without a flicker of warning, the words will begin to collide like a freeway pileup. Imagine being sleepy so early in the evening! For a fleeting moment you'll remember how you used to walk under an April moon and wish that midnight would never come. All of a sudden it will hit you: In marriage it isn't always spring!

This is the unmasked reality that every couple eventually faces. True, some couples make the adjustment less painfully than others, but no couple avoids it completely. Be encouraged by that.

Rollie and I still have the postcard I sent to my parents thirty years ago. They saved it for us because of its rare combination of humor and naivete: "Bliss! Nothing but bliss! Day after day of uninterrupted bliss!"

I wrote that sentimental bit of melodrama after we had given our marriage the long enduring test of—eleven days.

But one sullen day about eleven weeks later, while rain was pouring like sheets of liquid glass, I pulled a crusted rack out of a crusted oven, stumbled over the dustpan in the middle of the floor, banged my head on an open cupboard door, and said aloud to the daisies on our wallpaper, "So *this*—is *bliss?*"

Was our marriage a tragic mistake? Was the excitement and joy of our engagement an illusive dream? Did crusted racks and dirty clothes and pressured schedules prove we didn't love each other? Were we "incompatible"?

No, Julie. It simply proved we had a lot to learn. We were beginning to discover what love and marriage were all about. We had committed ourselves to something far more inclusive than either of us had dared to dream. You and Kent will make the same discovery.

Remember the books I've loaned you by Sam Shoemaker? Somewhere in one of them he points out that everybody *has* a problem, *is* a problem, or *lives* with a problem. We can't argue that!

So one thing is certain: Whatever marriage was meant to be, it wasn't meant to be easy. Any theory about marriage which ignores stark reality isn't worth considering. In other words, there are problems.

Take a quick look at the problems you'll tackle in the day-after-day routine: the spotted toilet, the greasy stove, the refrigerator with the strange sour odor drifting from somewhere, and two squashed tomatoes in the vegetable bin.

Take a glance at the unpolished silver, the undusted furniture, the drooping plants that need water. The sticky syrup on your carpeting, the spoon caught in the disposal, the delicate china cup shattered before your eyes, the termite pellets on the closet shelf.

In marriage it isn't always spring!

But that's only part of the scene. You both may have jobs, so on foggy mornings you'll battle traffic and cautiously switch lanes and hope you can show up at the office before your boss arrives. While you creep with the traffic you'll think about mounting bills and the laundry you forgot to transfer to the dryer and the meat you should have taken out of the freezer.

In marriage there are sudden emergencies, too: a crushed fender which was undoubtedly your fault. A plugged disposal on the Saturday night you're having two couples for dinner. A telephone call in the middle of the night—your mother is suddenly terribly ill and your dad doesn't know what to do.

There are overprotective relatives and neighbors with silly complaints. Tempers flare and words slash and tears spill all over the place. Hostilities crouch in corners. *It isn't so much what we say to each other,* you think secretly, *it's the tone we use when we say it.*

Once in a while you can't help it. Pictures will shape and dissolve in your mind. You'll think back to the simple, carefree days when you came and went as you pleased, when the money you earned was yours, when you didn't worry if a button was missing. Unmatched socks didn't bother you either—that was your dad's problem.

When you wanted to get away from your family you put the Do Not Disturb sign on your bedroom door, or you dashed into the kitchen, grabbed a cookie, and said, "Gotta run, mom."

But when you're married, it's different. You're accountable to each other. You're responsible. You're making a life investment in a permanent relationship. *Your* way becomes *our* way. *Earned* money is *joint* money. *My* time is *shared* time. On the run means off to work and home to work.

In marriage it isn't always spring!

Does that disturb you, Julie? It needn't! Every season is beautiful, *and the secret of the seasons is balance.* Every marriage needs the tranquillity of winter, the warmth of summer, the brilliance of autumn, the exuberance of spring.

Without dishes and dusting we'd miss the discipline. Without conflicts we'd miss compromises. Without problems we'd miss prayer. Without hurting we'd miss holding. Without listening we'd miss learning. Without grief we'd miss growth. Without the darkness we'd miss the dawn.

Love is not endless bliss. It is not continued ecstasy. It is not Hawaii in May and Palm Springs in December. Love is genuinely wanting the highest and best for your mate—as much as you want it for yourself. It doesn't happen all at once. We learn it by living it. That's what marriage is all about.

Many times I'm plodding when I'd rather soar, or I'm pulling weeds when I'd rather be swinging on a star, or I'm submerged in soapsuds when I'd love to be watching the whitecaps dash against the sandy shore.

Or at least I think I would. When it comes right down to it, I wouldn't trade my lot with all the queens who ever lived, nor would I trade my home for a palace. Why should I?

In one of your recent letters you wrote something very significant: "Kent and I are slowly learning to know the real persons behind the stars in our eyes, and the neat thing is—the stars are still shining."

Julie, I wish I could frame that sentence in gold for your first home. I know of no finer definition for the word *balance* as it pertains to marriage.

God has a lot of stars up there, Julie! He's willing to share them as long as you'll let him.

From My Journal
Marriage is a combination of salt and stardust—salt for hamburgers and stardust for poetry. You can undoubtedly survive a little longer on hamburgers than you can on poetry; but why settle for one when God wants you to have both?

Voices from the Past

Dear Julie,

If Kent doesn't happen to like cottage cheese *before* you're married, he isn't likely to eat it with gusto two days after your honeymoon.

If he's never given a thought to size 11 shoes kicked under the bed, take it in stride the first time your new vacuum tangles with shoelaces.

If you've never cleaned a refrigerator (lots of brides haven't), it won't suddenly seem as easy as apple pie after your honeymoon. Then again it might—if you've never baked an apple pie!

It is vitally important that you remember one solid fact: *Basically, you will both be exactly the same persons after your wedding as you were before.* The ceremony, with all its shimmering beauty, will not magically make two *imperfect* people *perfect.*

A thoughtful wife said one day, "I had no idea we'd hear so many voices from the past after our wedding. All of our conditioning, our moods, our clinging habits just moved right in with us—rent-free!"

Julie, in every marriage there are inescapable voices from the past. At times they whisper; often they shout.

But if you hear them with openness and gentle love, they need not damage your relationship. Actually they will push you on toward maturity. This is God's intention! So let's look together at these voices.

- *The voice of established patterns.*

I have a friend whose family celebrates big—they always have. Parties, picnics, the works. On her first married birthday her husband gave her a tube of pink lipstick and a card—that was it. A very ordinary day.

She chided herself for her disappointment. When she told me about it, she said, "It wasn't that I wanted an expensive gift—I just missed a real celebration."

But later her husband said with glowing pride, "Honey, I hope the lipstick was all right. That's the first time in my life I gave anyone a birthday gift. In my family we didn't even give cards."

- *The voice of hidden traits.*

Living together day-in-day-out is a revealing experience. We see each other without facade or pretense. The true self emerges. We begin to recognize traits we hadn't detected before—an assertiveness, perhaps, or stifling fear. We see temper, impatience, hostility. We see blunder and bluff. Lack of discipline becomes obvious. Often we see deep conflicts between will and emotion, between duty and desire. "For better or for worse" become words of stark reality.

- *The voice of moods, habits, and manners.*

Emotions are incredibly puzzling. Moods sweep us rapidly from the basement of despair to the tenth floor of exhilaration.

A meticulous bride said, "An open closet door just makes me furious!" Sometimes it doesn't take much. Habits and manners can be as irritating as tiny gnats. Lost keys, newspaper clutter, towels heaped in a corner, nervous gestures, too much food in one busy mouth, elbows slumped over the table . . .

Voices from the past!

Julie, marriage is not a game for children. Without a doubt, you will find the pressures after marriage bigger than any you have encountered before.

At first you'll be tempted to treat the voices as uninvited guests. You'll hedge. You'll ignore them. At times you'll retreat. You'll run to the bedroom and close the door, or you'll dash out of the house, or you'll jump into the car and drive for an hour.

But they won't budge!

Your next tactic will be force. You'll shout, you'll cry, you'll mix plaintive pleas with exaggerated gestures.

Again it won't work. You see, the voices will *like* living in your cozy home. They've known you both for a long time.

Is there a solution, then? How can you learn to "live happily ever after" with such brazen interference in your home? Let me suggest several ways:

● *Introduce each voice to Jesus Christ, your invited Friend.*

He alone can handle the conflicts. His love transforms. His power recreates. He will begin to mold and sharpen and refashion. He will teach you to make friends with the voices. Gradually you will discover a refreshing fact: Your strengths are supporting each other's weaknesses!

● *Refuse to let the voices drown out the verbal expression of love.*
"Honey, I just want to thank you for your increased patience. I've really noticed it. I love being married to you!"

"You *look* nice, sound nice, smell nice . . . well, you're just plain nice! I love sleeping with you!"

"Wow! We haven't quarreled about money for a month. Am I doing better? Shall we visit your parents tonight? I just noticed something . . . you have very nice ears!"

"You know what? I think we're growing up!"

- *Demonstrate love when you don't feel loving.*

One day I had a telephone call. A charming voice on the other end of the line said, "We're delighted that you're going to speak at our potluck tomorrow night. Do you need a ride?"

I was dumbfounded. *Nobody* had called me about speaking at a potluck dinner! As it happened, Rollie had taken the message. Rollie had graciously accepted the invitation for me on a tentative basis. (I was to call back if I couldn't speak.) Rollie had neglected to tell me.

At that precise moment I didn't exactly feel like writing a love letter. But had anyone asked, "Do you love your husband?" my immediate response would have been, "I certainly do! If I didn't, you'd never catch me in a predicament like this!"

- *Accept each other realistically.*

Often we have faced ourselves with definite questions:

Is this really important enough to make an issue over?

Do I want this change for my own ego needs, or for the good of my mate and his outside relationships?

How could I have handled this conflict more tactfully and maturely?

As I pray about us, am I determining God's answer before I really know it?

Is this a trait I should accept unconditionally, or may I anticipate God's creative change?

If my mate's reaction were the same as mine at this instant, would I feel hurt or resentful?

- *Let laughter lighten the load.*

Laughter is a beautiful thing! It looks like a rainbow. It sounds like a mountain stream. It feels like a refreshing shower. It softens our moods, sweetens our dispositions, sustains us when the going is rough. Learn to laugh together!

- *Don't expect a perfect marriage.*

There is only one way your marriage can be at least fifty percent perfect: when *you* reach the state of perfection. That's about as close as you'll get. I've never yet seen a perfect husband!

- *Be consistently grateful.*

You can change! The process may be long, even tedious, but the Great Designer knows what he's about. What we have been need never be as mighty as what we may become. We cooperate in God's molding process not by nagging, but by nurturing. Not by needling, but by kneeling. Not by deflating, but by praising. So thank God for every evidence of growth.

Just one final reminder, Julie: Whatever secret irritations you discover in each other before your marriage, begin now to accept them with genuine love and understanding.

Find Your Own Hilltop

Dear Julie,

If I were asked what I consider the greatest cementing force in our marriage, I would not say, "Well, you see it's like this—we try to compliment each other every day. We share the work load; we talk things over." Nor would I say, "Rollie always opens the car door for me. We light a candle at the dinner table. . . . "

All of these things have their place, and they do enhance a marriage relationship when love, not manipulation, is the motive.

But the one consistent habit above all others that has drawn us closer to each other and to God is this: From the beginning of our marriage we've kept prayer high on our priority list. We've prayed *for* and *with* each other for thirty years.

Our day always starts with a cup of coffee and a few delicious morsels from the Bible. (Breakfast after that!) We've discovered that it's better to read five or ten verses and digest them than to attempt three chapters haphazardly. We pray specifically. We ask God to enable us to apply what we've read as we face the demands of the new day.

Often we pray aloud as we walk together—in the rain or under the smiling sun. I remember the sense of oneness we felt with our entire neighborhood the day we took turns praying for families whose homes we passed. We asked God to resolve conflicts and give guidance to parents and children. As we prayed for each marriage, we felt a sudden closeness toward mates who may never have prayed for each other.

Sometimes we pray while driving. As we share our personal longings and needs, Rollie's hand always reaches for mine. The sense of God's presence is awesome. We *know* he's riding with us.

Once or twice we've stopped pulling weeds in our backyard. Under a hot August sun we've asked God to clear the choking weeds from our hearts and to make our lives a productive garden.

We even sing our prayers! I was struggling with a personal conflict one day. I wanted God's will, but I wanted my will, too. I knew the controversy would have to be decided in God's favor. He was waiting! The old hymn "Have Thine Own Way, Lord" pushed into my thoughts. We sang it together: "Mold me and make me, after thy will. . . . " The song became the prayer that brought a settled release.

We've sometimes roared with laughter when words haven't come out right—when crazy sentences sounded just so ridiculous. I think God, who gave the gift of laughter, laughed with us!

Sometimes we've held each other and wept in the middle of a prayer. Rollie apologized one day for his silent tears. But Jesus wept!

In Palm Springs there's a very special swimming pool. It doesn't look much different from a hundred other pools, but one September afternoon, surrounded by splashing vacationers, we talked to God in that pool! We quietly thanked him for the glorious vacation he had given us—so relaxing, just what we needed.

Several years have passed since we found our private hill. The very first night we claimed it as our own—our hilltop oasis. Every so often, when pressures tighten their grip, when our attitudes need revamping, we find our way over the winding road to our private hilltop. We look down over a vast expanse of shimmering lights, a veritable wonderland. With the stars shining above, we feel suspended somewhere between earth and heaven.

The top of our hill is our Center of Silence. It is here that we pray for the people we love most. It is here that we recapture the incredible joy of abandonment to God.

Julie, if I could make a wish, it would be this: that you and Kent might discover the ever-deepening enrichment of sharing *everything* with God.

I know that most people have questions about prayer. We do, too. Admittedly there is an overwhelming vastness to its implications. We're mystified about guidance, about unanswered prayer, about God's will. All of us stumble over our doubts at crucial times.

But one thing we've learned in our marriage: When we determine to talk *with* God rather than *about* him; when we go to him as our loving Father, simply because Jesus told us to, something happens in our lives and in our marriage.

"How do we start praying when we've never prayed together?" This is a typical question asked by many couples. I understand it so well. Although family worship was a daily pattern in our family, I suddenly realized after we were married that I'd never prayed with a *husband* before. Rollie had never prayed with a *wife* before. This was a new kind of intimacy. Were we willing for this transparency in our marriage?

Yes, we decided, we were. Our love was deep and real, and we wanted God to be *first* in our home. So we began to pray, each in his own faltering way, with hesitant words and clumsy rhetoric. Short prayers. Jumbled thoughts. But we kept at it until praying together became a joyous adventure.

Now let me suggest several things that I trust will make the beginning a little easier:

1. In an unhurried way, begin by expressing gratitude at mealtime. Bowed heads and clasped hands create a beautiful atmosphere of love and reverence. Take turns praying aloud. It needn't be a long prayer.

2. Occasionally, try writing your prayer requests. Then as you exchange lists, pray silently (or audibly if you can!) for each other.

3. Pray sometimes without asking for anything. Just praise God as you wait silently in his presence.

4. Pray conversationally, each a sentence or two about one subject. Talk to God personally and unpretentiously.

5. Be specific and expectant. He hears you!

6. Listen to God! Prayer is two-way communication. God speaks in many ways, but most consistently through the Bible. Find your own method of study. We like to alternate—a book in the New Testament and then one in the Old. Circle, underline, write on margins. Share your thoughts with each other.

7. When you don't feel like praying, don't give up! Tell God about it. As a mother smiles her baby into smiling, he will love you into praying.

The other day a young wife said to me, "Ruth, I'm sure my husband would never pray with me. He'd be embarrassed. He says prayer is a personal matter."

So I told her about our friends, Betty and Bill.

When Betty called me several months ago, I knew something tremendous had happened the minute she said hello. She couldn't spill the news fast enough.

"Ruth, the most exciting thing is happening in our home. For the first time in thirty-three years Bill and I are praying together! We actually kneel by the bed and pray aloud. It's making everything different. We can't catch the miracles fast enough."

Betty and Bill had been Christians for years. They had raised two beautiful children and had still found time for numerous community causes: school boards, election boards, church boards. They had worked hard and they had reached some lofty goals.

But now their children were grown. Parental tasks no longer demanded time and energy. They began to reevaluate, to check priorities. In a way, it meant learning to know and accept each other all over again. They needed to talk to God *together*.

And so one day it happened! After thirty-three years they knelt together and prayed aloud. They were little children again, coming to their Father! And now he is working in their lives in ways they had never dreamed. "If it can happen to us," Betty told me that day, "it can happen to anyone!"

We have a Father. And a father's counsel always comes through best to children who trust!

Lord, Please Whisper a Secret

Dear Julie,

It's a magnificent thing to carry on a personal correspondence with the God of the Universe! I've been doing it for years. Let me tell you about it.

I was probably eight or nine when my father called me into his study one day. In simple language, he explained to a little girl God's methods of communication—how he speaks to us through the Bible, through books and music and sermons, through people and circumstances; how he whispers secrets to anyone who will listen. I was fascinated! To think that the God who made the stars and sky and rushing seas would actually talk to me!

Dad told me that he often wrote down the thoughts that seemed to come from God as he prayed and read and studied. I was immensely challenged. *I wanted to hear secrets!* So that very week a little blue notebook became a book of secret prayers—childish, but honest. For example:

> Dear Jesus,
>
> Today you whispered a secret. I told a lie to my mother, and you said to say I'm sorry. Now I have a secret for you. I don't want to tell her yet, so please don't tell her before I do.

That was the beginning, Julie. Since then I have filled many notebooks—red, blue, green, and yellow—with intimate thoughts expressed directly to God. There are several reasons why this practice has been profoundly valuable:

1. My attention is focused on God. There is not the muddled distraction of the tilted lamp shade, the crooked picture, the piece of lint on the carpeting.

2. Distorted thoughts are crystallized and expressed coherently. I do not rely on the same ragged ''bless me'' platitudes.

3. A written prayer is a personal commitment not easily ignored or forgotten. God often reminds me of my written communication.

4. As my sensitivity deepens, I am continually amazed at God's direct (and sometimes immediate) response to my heart's deep petitions.

From time to time I have shared this method of prayer with close friends. A letter from my friend Janet says:

> Dear Ruth,
> I am recalling the days when I sat at your piano learning chords and arpeggios, but learning so much more, too. As much as I enjoy music, perhaps your greatest contribution to my life began the day you taught me to write my thoughts and longings to God, then to listen with pen in hand as the Holy Spirit reveals the will of the Father.
> And now as a wife and mother, I daily meet challenges which are fully faced through this precious avenue of communion. When frustrations mount, he gives me wisdom I can refer to again and again.
> Thanks for a gift which will have lasting and growing fulfillment all the days of my life.
>
> Love,
> Janet

Julie, I share Janet's letter to encourage you to find the tremendous spiritual stimulus that comes from spending time alone with God in a personal encounter. We need to pray with our mates, but we need to pray alone, too.

I'm sending some thoughts from my own notebooks—picked at random—to show you the simplicity of the plan.

Launch out on the joy of an intriguing experiment. Pour out your heart to God, then open the windows and God will do the rest. He is always waiting to give us himself!

Lord, today I wish I were a cheerleader waving colorful pompons! I'd march through the streets of our town and shout a tribute to the majesty of God. Everybody in the world ought to be singing the "Hallelujah Chorus" on a morning like this. All of nature exalts you—from the newest blade of grass to the tallest oak. And I? Well, I tingle all over with the wonder of it all!

* * *

Today, dear Lord, I asked you how I could know if my surrender was complete. You said so simply, "How is it with you now—this moment? Settle it each moment, and you won't need to ask."

* * *

Lord, yesterday at the sunny beach I traced little lines in the sand with a small twig. The wet spray blew against my face, and a thousand thoughts went tumbling into the waves. When I talked to you I heard you say, "My boundless love surrounds you . . . ."

Today I am at home again—fixing meals, washing dishes, talking on the phone, answering mail—all the ordinary things, Lord. When I talk to you I hear you say, "My boundless love surrounds you."

And, dear God, suddenly I know it is as true today as it was yesterday!

Forgiveness Is a Beautiful Word

Dear Julie,
Have I ever told you about Faye?

Years ago, when our family lived in Chicago, Faye and I were best friends. We walked to school together five mornings a week. We giggled and jumped rope and exchanged favorite books. We shared hair clips and diary secrets. Ours was a friendship of utter devotion.

When we were in the fifth grade, a lanky, blue-eyed boy stumbled (literally) over my desk one day. He was pretty ho-hum, certainly no pacesetter, but he liked me and said so.

One day he handed me a note. "I like you, you're nice." Julie, the room turned upside down! I could hardly wait for the bell to ring. I *had* to ask Faye to be my maid-of-honor in ten years.

Then, out of the blue, the boy (I don't remember his name) discovered Faye. She was prettier than I, and far more adept at arithmetic. Result? In the middle of long-range wedding plans I lost the boy, and Faye lost her best friend.

Our friendship was shattered. We passed each other on the school grounds without a word. Our mutual friends begged us to make up, but we refused. Our alienation continued even after the boy was no longer important.

But finally at the end of the year, a week before summer vacation, Faye knocked at our back door. She said pleadingly, "Let's make up—please! You're still my very best friend."

Everything loving inside me wanted desperately to throw my arms around her. I ached to say, "You're my best friend, too!" But everything stubborn and selfish and cruel inside me refused to acknowledge love. I'd been hurt, and I assumed the frightening responsibility of punishing Faye.

When I saw her pushing back tears, I finally said, "Our family is going on vacation when school is out. *Maybe* I'll make up when we get home." Faye walked slowly toward her home—I can still picture her crossing the street . . . .

We were gone three weeks—three miserable I-don't-like-me weeks. We hadn't been home more than five minutes before I rushed to the phone. My heart pounded. I *had* to talk to Faye. I wanted to shout at the top of my lungs, "You're my best friend, you really are!"

But Faye didn't answer the phone. A strange, unfamiliar voice said, "The Kimballs have left town—I don't have their address."

Julie, my heart stood still. I'm not even sure if I said good-bye. I've suffered many times since that moment, but never in quite the same way.

I've never seen Faye since the day she knocked at our door asking for my forgiveness. But often through the years I've thanked God for engraving upon my young heart a lesson I've never forgotten.

Someone said one day, "But you were so young, and it was just a little thing!" No, Julie—unforgiveness is never a little thing. It warps and shrivels our souls. It boxes us in and often it tears hearts and homes apart. It stands as an immovable boulder when we try to pray. *We just have to forgive.*

You're probably thinking, "Did your childhood experience eliminate every future struggle? Is forgiveness always an easy thing for you now?"

Julie, not for a moment am I suggesting that all grievances are as simple as a fifth-grade love affair. Often forgiveness seems utterly impossible—*is* impossible, in fact, apart from God's grace.

Countless individuals have endured agonizing injustice. We do cruel and vicious things to each other. Hundreds of homes are saturated with grievances. Often family members are demolished by unkind put-downs. Husbands and wives become victims of infidelity or neglect or unconcern. Sarcasm and ridicule can be so slashing. Forgiveness is *not* always an easy thing.

Many times I hurt. I am a sensitive person—at times *touchy* might be a better word! I feel things deeply. Words and actions cut. My inclination is to brood, to "suffer silently." But one truth is deeply ingrained within me:

There is no hurt, no offense, no agony too great for God to heal! Whatever the cutting pain, the demeaning injustice, the love of Jesus can withstand it! When we *ask* for the gift of forgiveness, God always says yes!

Forgiveness does not mean that we disregard an offense. To say, "Don't worry, it's all right," is often less than honest. Many things are far from all right.

Forgiveness simply means a deliberate release of an offense. We *choose* to forgive! We *accept,* we *release,* and we *drop the charges*—just as God, through Jesus Christ, dropped ALL charges against us. The enabling power comes from him!

Forgiveness frees us from our subjectivity. We no longer wince or wallow in self-pity. We may *remember* at times (forgiveness may not always mean forgetting), but we are confident that God is weaving every memory into his glorious pattern. His redemptive love covers our memories!

To ask for forgiveness is the other side of the coin. Often it's easier to say, "I want to take you to dinner" or "I bought you a gift" or "I have a funny story to tell you" than to say, "I was wrong."

You see, Julie, when we apologize we do battle with our pride. But real healing cannot begin until we acknowledge our offense. To attempt to erase the hurt engendered by sarcasm or crushing ridicule is like splashing on perfume before a shower on a hot, humid day. The offense becomes more repulsive. We need cleansing! We need to be forgiven.

And sometimes we need to help each other apologize.

My father often told a story of a husband who had deeply hurt his wife. Yet he found it insuperably difficult to say, "I'm sorry." As a child he had been forced to apologize for offenses he had not committed. The experience had damaged him emotionally.

The wife, understanding her husband's need, longed to help him. Finally, with her arms around him, she said gently, "Your eyes have that beautiful 'I'm sorry' look. I just want you to know that I completely forgive you!"

Forgiveness is a beautiful word!

I'm sure you remember the popular sentence, "Love is never having to say you're sorry." Thousands of people grabbed hold of that when they read or heard it the first time. It needs just one change to make it true: Change the words *never having* to *being able*. Isn't that a more solid definition?

Remember, Julie, the important thing in your marriage is always to make things right again. There *must* be a restored relationship. You have to look straight at the wrong, as Paul Tournier says, *see* it as wrong, and then forgive it. Sometimes you may even have to ask, "Will you give me the joy of forgiving you?" Why wait? Why build a wall around yourself? Why endure the fatigue and isolation and self-reproach that unforgiveness brings? Why put off what must be done eventually if healing is to take place? God's gift of forgiveness is free for the asking!

Years ago, when I told Rollie about my friend Faye, he said, "Honey, let's never wait to forgive." We promised that we'd never go to sleep angry at each other. We've kept our word! Once or twice we've stayed awake until 5:00 A.M. getting things settled, but it usually happened to be at a time when we could sleep a little in the morning!

Our pastor, Dr. Ted Cole, often says, "Keep short accounts with God." That helps me so much. You see, there is simply no way I can keep short accounts with God and keep long accounts with the members of his family. None of us can. Jesus said so first: "Forgive, and you shall be forgiven."

Forgiveness is a beautiful word!

From My Journal
There is no hurt worth
clinging to
When I love you as I do!

We Must Get Together Sometime

Dear Julie,
Let's talk about hospitality!

The first week we moved into our first *real* home, we had a party—even before we were half settled. We just couldn't wait! God had been good to us, and we wanted to celebrate. Everything was pretty helter-skelter, dozens of things we needed were still missing, but nobody noticed—nobody cared.

Laughter and singing flooded every room. Ideas were sprouting everywhere: "Hey, you could hang your big mirror over the couch!"

"How about putting the maple rocker in the corner over there?"

"You could use an extra shelf or two in that closet."

Suggestions were frequent and free; we could take them or leave them. We were sharing God's goodness, and our hearts were throbbing with joy.

After hot chocolate and peanut butter cookies, Rollie sang with gusto the old familiar song "Bless This House." I secretly smiled, *Yes, Lord, please do!*

A little later we formed a circle of prayer—all of us—in the cluttered room, and everybody took turns praying. We dedicated our home to God—every room, every piece of furniture, even the future possibilities. Our home was his love-gift to us. Best of all, he lived with us!

My parents were with us that night. I'll never forget my father's prayer. It hit the target of my heart: "Lord, may everyone who enters this house learn a little more of your love—just by being here!"

Julie, that's what hospitality is all about: God's love extended through us, where we live—in a single room or in a palatial mansion.

Hospitality starts with a wide-open door, a wide-open heart, a friendly smile. Hospitality says, "We care about you and we want you to know."

Any corner of the house is fair game for hospitality—a crowded kitchen, a candlelit table with a lovely lace cloth, a flickering fireside, a patio on a warm August night. The setting almost always takes more imagination than money. It's the small, intimate touches that make for friendship and festivity, in August or December.

At our house friends often eat from wooden bowls, bean pots, soup mugs, or paper plates. We've had company for breakfast early in the morning. We've had midmorning brunches and salad buffets and indoor picnics and waffle suppers and after-church chili feeds. Our patio comes alive with sizzling hamburgers and roasted wieners and sizable servings of spicy spaghetti.

Sometimes a dozen friends sing their hearts out around our piano. Nobody ever wants to stop singing! Almost always we end the evening with crunchy apples and buttered popcorn—that's all.

Often on guest nights we have soup and salad—and a fruit

cup for dessert. Does it sound meager? Well, I make a *lot* of soup! We even play games occasionally. One night somebody said, "I haven't had so much fun since I was a kid!" Nobody *has* to play. They can read if they'd rather.

Have you ever heard of graham crackers and spiced tea for refreshments? It happens at our house! Sometimes I frost the graham crackers. I light candles, too.

Gourmet dinners? Once in a while, but not often. Not anymore. You should have seen me entertain in the early years of our marriage. Fun? No, frantic. Delightful? No, demolishing.

I'd rush from morning until dinnertime. I'd plan elaborate five-course dinners with five forks at each plate. Nobody knew when to use them. I didn't either, but they looked *so* impressive. We'd never have more than two couples at a time—just couldn't! Not enough money (or forks). Exhaustion always numbed me.

"Mother never told me entertaining would be like this," I'd wail. We'd always had company in our old-fashioned parsonages. It seemed so easy—for mother!

One early morning while I was baking a peach cobbler for company, God caught me right in the middle of my muddle. He pointedly asked, "Do you want to *impress,* or do you want to *express* my love?" The question jolted me. I couldn't evade it. The sad truth was—I wanted to impress. Result: drudgery. Frayed nerves. A litany of lament.

Starting that very day, God slowly revamped my perspective. The word *simplicity* covered me like a soft blanket. A mellow truth took hold of my heart: Jesus would have been pleased with crackers and cheese, had Martha joined Mary at his feet. I began to discover that the more simply I served, the more compassionately I cared.

71

Today, the walls of our house could tell a thousand secrets. Between bites and sips we've laughed and cried. We've shared ridiculous jokes and shining memories. We've had challenging discussions; we've expressed creative ideas. We've prayed—how often we've prayed!

One day my friend Donna said, "Ruth, it's funny, but I never seem to remember how your house looks when I leave. All I can think about is how warm and loved I feel when I'm there." All that day I thanked God for teaching me something about expressing his love.

Julie, you don't have to be a creative genius to make your guests feel warm and wanted. You need never apologize for a home in which Jesus Christ delights to live. Simply expose your friends—and strangers, too—to love, to caring. Help them to feel relaxed. Guests should never have to feel they're being graded for social etiquette. Let your entertaining be vibrant yet casual. Try to create a feeling of leisure and comfort. If you're dividing your time between home and office, all the more reason for *simplicity.*

Once in a while it's fun to go all out with something daring—even if you chance a catastrophe. But you'd be wise to try your not-so-sure ideas when you're having friends who'll laugh with you and understand no matter how things turn out.

Give yourself the joy of inviting someone for dinner who could never reciprocate. I can't begin to tell you the delightful times we've had entertaining people who we *knew* could never return the invitation.

Don't apologize for a dry roast or too much salt or a gelatin salad that didn't quite congeal. Chances are your guests won't even notice—so don't remind them. When it's time for compliments, accept them graciously.

There will be times when you'll be tempted to say, "I'll never have company again!" But you will. At least I hope so! Maybe you can't always be the best cook in your circle of friends, but one thing you *can* do: You can open your heart as wide as you open your front door. You can express God's love. You can radiate the compassion of Jesus Christ.

With every act of kindness you can say, "We care about you and we want you to know!"

"Be hospitable to each other without secretly wishing you hadn't got to be!" (I Pet. 4:9, Phillips). That says it best of all!

Love Letters and Secret Signals

Dear Julie,

Rollie and I are dyed-in-the-wool note writers. Actually, with all the notes we've written over the years, we've probably made a sizable contribution to the paper shortage.

Note writing for me started years ago—long before I met my husband. I grew up just naturally assuming that all families everywhere wrote notes. What else were scratch pads for? Note writing was an accepted part of life—like drinking milk, like jumping rope.

We all remember, in our family, the notes mother used to tuck inside our lunch pails. (Sacks didn't happen to be "in" when we were in school.) Three minutes after the lunch bell clanged, we'd open our sturdy lunch pails, hungry as could be, and sure enough—nestled neatly between a juicy red apple and a peanut butter sandwich, we'd find a personal note. Each one added a few musical grace notes to our day. We felt very—*special*.

Since I was brought up on more notes than Pablum, it seemed the most natural thing in the world to write love notes to Rollie when we began dating seriously. His echoing response was marvelous. We've been writing ever since.

I'm certainly aware that love letters are not a new idea. But what would happen, I wonder, if husbands and wives would continue to express surges of warmth and appreciation long *after* the wedding—love notes translated into action.

At our house note writing falls into categories. I'm going to share a few tucked-away notes with you. We write . . .

Instructive Notes:
Honey, if you get home first, please put the round casserole in the oven at 350 degrees. The casserole is in the refrigerator. I think you'll like dinner tonight. (Do you like me? Why? I can tell you a thousand reasons why I like you. Got time?)

Appreciation Notes:
Wow! The yard looks beautiful. I didn't dream you'd do all that weeding. Thanks, sweetheart. I'm *never* going to trade you in!

Reminder Notes:
Honey, be sure to be here when the repair man comes to fix the machine. He said he'd be here this afternoon, but he couldn't give me a definite time.

I-Need-You-So Notes:
Honey, for some reason this is such a difficult day for me. I can't explain it, but everything has gone wrong at the office. I can always sense the difference when you pray, so I'm counting on you. Thanks!

I'm-So-Sorry Notes:
I'm so sorry! I know I hurt you today. I'm sure now that we should have talked it over before I made the decision. It's too late for that, so I'm just asking you to forgive me . . . please? You know I never want to hurt you.

While-You're-Away Notes:
   Please know I'll be loving you all the while you're gone. I won't forget our special time at 10:00. Our house is so small, but it always seems so HUGE when you're away. Hurry!

Notes can be hidden almost anywhere: in the refrigerator, under pillows, in the driver's seat of the car, in pockets, in dresser drawers, even in the cookie jar! But they don't have to be hidden at all. It's great fun to find a note at the breakfast table, or dinner table, right next to your coffee cup, or in the bedroom on top of your dresser or desk.

   I love to send love notes to Rollie at his office, and once in a while he dashes off a quickie to me—the kind you don't dictate to a secretary.

   Do we write every day? Of course not. That could get tiresome, and it's freshness we're after! We have no absolutes about love notes. There are days when we're rushing too fast to scratch a single scribble. However, I doubt that a week has gone by at our house without several short notes left here and there. Often we've found them just when we needed them most!

   Notes travel on the same path with secret signals like gentle pats and telephone calls and holding hands in the car and touching fingers in a crowd and saying *I love you* with a silly cough that nobody else recognizes . . . .

   So much in marriage depends on big things, but so much depends on little things, too—like . . . well, like love notes! Any old scratch pad will do. Be sure to keep a big supply on hand!

Listening Love

Dear Julie,

Last Sunday afternoon, on our way home from a chapel wedding, Rollie and I noticed the dark, oppressive sky. It had been a glorious morning—spring at its brilliant best—so the sudden change was startling.

Rollie always likes to know what's going on—I could just see the wheels turning. I wasn't at all surprised when he said, "Let's check it out—it could be a fire!"

We drove four or five miles before discovering the clues: two fire engines, a wide-open field filled with smoldering debris, puffs of smoke—still whirling. The fire was obviously controlled, so we started toward home.

But for some reason, I just couldn't forget that smoldering field. Nor could I forget the words that prompted our unexpected detour: *"Let's check it out–it could be a fire!"*

I pictured a wide-open field called Communication. I thought of the smoldering debris of misunderstanding clouding so many marriages.

I thought of smoking embers—embers of self-pity and sophisticated facades . . . .

Of suave tones and surface talk and icy silences . . .

Of monologues . . . bargaining sessions . . . cutoffs . . .
defenses . . .

I thought of set jaws and tight fists and angry eyes . . .

And then I thought of *listening love*—the most treasured gift
a husband and wife can give to each other!

So today, Julie, let's check out the happy clues of listening
love—clues that lead to deeper understanding and continual
growth!

1. *Listening love is courteous. It says* . . .

I will strive to not interrupt or correct or outguess you. I
will not finish your sentences. I will not anticipate or break into
your thoughts with "instant solutions." I will not embarrass
you by "explaining" your comments in the presence of others.

2. *Listening love is attentive. It says* . . .

I will give you my full, undivided attention. I will not turn
you off. I will not walk out on you, or hide behind a smiling
mask. I will not leave you isolated. I will not busy myself with
trivials. I will strive to make our confrontation eye-to-eye,
heart-to-heart, and love-to-love.

3. *Listening love is kind. It says* . . .

I will not overwhelm you with harsh, sarcastic retorts. I will
not belittle or rebuke you. I will avoid unqualified terms like
"you never . . ." and "you always . . . ." I will strive to bring
healing out of hurt, laughter out of tears, and understanding
out of contention.

4. *Listening love is objective. It says* . . .

I will not attempt to *think* for you. I will strive to be
informative rather than opinionated. I will not disagree with
what you say until I am reasonably sure I understand what you
mean.

5. *Listening love is patient. It says . . .*

I will not rush you. I will not insist on a right-now conclusion. I will recognize the fact that two distinct opinions do not necessarily mean that one of us is wrong.

6. *Listening love is sensitive. It says . . .*

I will strive to listen to what you *do not* say—the feelings behind the words. I will attempt to "say back" what you have said, as I understand it. If, at a given moment, you cannot express your deep feelings, I will wait for you—as I would want you to wait for me.

7. *Listening love is unselfish. It says . . .*

I will guard against superconfidence, against pushy probing, against trite "spiritual answers," against wanting always to be right.

8. *Listening love is confidential. It says . . .*

I will never betray you. The secrets you have shared are locked in my heart. You alone know the combination.

9. *Listening love is prayerful. It says . . .*

Quietly, confidently, I will pray for insight, for wisdom, for tolerance. I will pray for the capacity to cope with the unpredictable. I will pray for gentle reactions. I will pray for sharing that does not count the cost or the return. I will pray above all for a love that intertwines with the love of God.

10. *Listening love is growing. It says . . .*

The more *dearly* I love you, the more *clearly* I hear you.

How does it come about, a breakdown in communication? Does it happen all at once? Like a sudden cyclone sweeping away words and glances and deep feelings?

No, Julie, not that way. It is more subtle than that—*much more.* It starts with little jabs, little rivalries, little revolts. It starts with wanting *my* way because how I feel is more important than how *you* feel. It starts with blaming each other until aloofness develops and pride takes over. Dialogue becomes monologue, and there is no freshness anymore, no frankness. There are no secrets that belong *just to us*. There is no transparency. Selfishness is an extremely lonely experience!

Your wedding will last an hour, but your marriage will last a lifetime. Marriage can be a whole lot of nice things, Julie—like sharing . . . giving . . . laughing . . . learning. . . . But if you lose out on communication, marriage can be a whole lot of miserable things—like rejection . . . competition . . . isolation . . . futility.

It is vitally important that you express your inner feelings and concerns to each other. You need to hear each other's voices and catch each other's smiles. And sometimes you need just plain ordinary chatter for a little while—without the burden of consuming problems! Wise old Solomon expressed it so aptly: "How wonderful it is to be able to say the right thing at the right time!" If you don't communicate about peripheral things, you will cheat yourselves out of the deeper experiences.

Last week I had lunch with my friend, Kelly. When Kelly sings and plays her guitar, I secretly glance around to be sure I'm still on earth. But Kelly and Ron would be the first to acknowledge that it takes more than a guitar to keep a marriage going.

"The thing I love about being married to Ron is that we talk about everything," Kelly told me. "That's what makes the difference for us. We've been married almost five years. Our temperaments are different, and we don't always agree on things. But we do talk, we share, and we know how we feel about each other."

Julie, at times you may grope to find the way. You may feel it's a dangerous thing to come out of your shells. In some very pertinent ways marriage is indeed a risk. Your coping abilities will be tested. You'll have to learn when to push a little, when to back off, when to start talking, when to say nothing.

Often you'll have to keep giving and giving until something breaks.

Then you'll have to keep giving until something heals.

In puzzling moments you may have to say, "Here we are, God, your little kids. Help us to grow up." *And then you'll have to grow up!* But everything will be all right as long as you can find a place to kneel. A three-way communication is the best guarantee for marriage at its best.

Yesterday a letter came from my friend, Kim. I want to share part of it with you. It expresses so beautifully what I've attempted to say.

> Sometimes I've tried to protect myself against hurt. But if you constantly cover your true feelings, it's like putting a drop-cloth over a beautiful chair . . . Sure, it won't get soiled, but you see only the form of the chair. You miss all the texture and beauty.
>
> I want to experience all my heavenly Father has for me, and I can't do that with a drop-cloth over my heart. So he'll just have to see that the paint-drips land in the right spots to blend with his pattern. I'm sure he will!
>
> Good-night,
> Kim

Christmas Heart-Gifts

Dear Julie,

As I write to you today, the golden sunlight streams through the windows, and the fragrance of spicy pine permeates our house. Wherever we look we see candles—on the stereo, the coffee table, the piano.

We never did get around to mending our half-demolished Christmas angel, the one with a broken wing and a tipped halo. She's more lopsided than ever this year. We smile every time we look at her.

Once or twice we talked about trading her in, but it was just a lot of talk. How could anybody reject an angel with a broken wing at Christmas time?

Our shimmering tree is the prettiest tree on the block—but only because it's ours. You'll understand that completely when you and Kent decorate your first tree. I get excited when I think of your first Christmas together and all the joy awaiting you.

Just think! Jesus was born in a stable, and God knew *then* that he'd be living in your home two millennia later. He certainly goes for long-range plans! Then he's got millions of little plans within the Big Plan—called *people*.

The other day when Rollie and I were out walking, we

stopped to talk to a pretty little girl who was sitting on her porch playing with her doll. This was the gist of our conversation:

"Why don't you tell your doll a story?"

"What kind of a story?"

"Well, why don't you tell her about God—how he made the trees and the mountains and the blue sky and . . . ."

"Hey, wait a minute, I know! Why don't I just tell her the *Jesus* story!"

Julie, that's what Christmas is all about. God breaking into history with his majestic power and unfathomable love to tell all the world the Jesus story.

Thank God for Christmas!

Thank God for joy!

I have Rollie's permission to send you a copy of the Christmas letter he wrote to me last year. Our Christmas letters have proved to be so enriching I thought the idea might be a challenge to you and Kent. Don't feel bound by it, however. I just like sharing ideas with you.

> Dear Mrs. Love,
> It's very late and you are asleep. I'll be there soon, but first I want to write my Christmas letter. You've probably written yours days ago!
>
> How long has this been going on now—our Christmas heart-gifts? Frankly, I don't remember when we started—eight years ago, maybe?
>
> I do remember the story you read aloud to me that Christmas Eve . . . about a couple who gave each other three heart-gifts each year. The idea challenged you. Right away you wanted to do it, too.
>
> When I saw how important it was to you, I finally agreed

to give it a whirl. So what happened? My letters are usually longer than yours!

This year, darling, I give you:

1. *The Gift of Do-It-Now.* Maybe that doesn't sound too exciting, but I remember November! You gave me a birthday card to mail to Aunt Martha. You had enclosed a small check, and you were anxious that she have it on time. Three days later you found the card on my desk under a newspaper. Well . . . I knew then what one of my heart-gifts would be!

The dripping faucet is another example. I'll never forget the day I walked into the kitchen and found you with a wrench in your hand tearing the plumbing apart. That just doesn't happen to be your talent!

2. *The Gift of Letting-You-Know.* This year I've been careless about passing on pertinent information. I remember your shock the day Lucille called to confirm a speaking engagement I had tentatively made for you. I probably shouldn't be mentioning this now, but you get the picture!

3. *The Gift of Laughter.* You said one day, "Honey, we've both been so pressured and serious about everything lately. I seldom hear you whistle anymore. We haven't had any real hysterics around here for a long time. Is it my fault?" I'll see if I can find my whistle again.

God is so good to us—just amazingly good! How I praise him for the gift of his Son, our Savior! We can never thank him quite sufficiently!

I know we said three gifts. But here again is the gift of my love.

Forever,
Rollie

If I Had Time...

Dear Julie,
Some wives are marvelously able to bounce out of bed in the morning all nice and smily while the sun is still yawning. My mother was like that. Every morning at six o'clock she'd be in the kitchen shuffling pots and pans, cheerful as could be.

I began to see early in our marriage (like about the third day) that it would be a long time before I'd win mother's trophy for discipline. I'd missed that word in a spelling contest once, and I was still struggling with it as a new bride. Most of my problems evolved around the management of time.

You should have seen me clean house! It wasn't that I minded the tedious work. I flew from kitchen to bedroom, from scrub cloth to dustcloth, from drawers to cupboards, from clean sheets to silver polish. First the broom, then the vacuum, here a little, there a little, never completing any job before starting something else. If all of this suggests some frightening neurotic tendencies, I obviously had them. But be encouraged, Julie. I've improved!

One day of utter confusion Rollie said, forcing a smile, "Honey, have you ever thought of making a list?" I was sure he meant a grocery list. My mind began racing—what in the world had I forgotten *this* time? But he was definitely talking about a time schedule. Slowly it began to dawn on me that I was sadly disorganized.

Several weeks later, while I was grating carrots for our dinner, I suddenly happened to remember a theme I had written in high school entitled, "If I Had Time." It was my teacher's comment, written neatly across the top of my paper, that left its indelible mark: "Why don't you *take* time?"

For the next hour or so I gave some serious thought to my poor planning and flimsy excuses. I realized that I could never box up time to save for a rainy day, nor could I retrieve it, or pull a weighty chunk of it back when it slipped from me.

Starting that night I began to write in my journal what God seemed to be saying to me regarding the sacred use of his gift of time. I'm sharing a few of the thoughts with you today, not because they are spectacular or tremendous or new, but because I believe the principles are valid:

Take time to . . .
Practice the presence of God. You are unique. God has made you different from anyone else for his own purpose. Don't copy; don't compete; don't be bound by the opinions of others. No one can determine God's schedule for you.

Take time to . . .
Plan your day wisely, under God's direction. (What thoughts come steadily, repeatedly, convincingly?) You can do everything you *ought* to do. Seek God's "oughts," then follow his guidance. Offer every responsibility, tiny or tremendous, as a love-gift to him.

90

Take time to . . .
Make realistic work lists. Discipline yourself. Avoid
procrastination. The key word is *Now*. Action creates feeling.
Work by a time schedule. Finish one task before starting
another. Don't ask for more time. But ask for wisdom to do in
the time you have what you *ought* to do.

Take time to . . .
Learn the warning signals: Are outside activities crowding
your marriage? Are you tense, indifferent, irritable? Are you
playing the martyr? Are you unforgiving? Are you careless
about your appearance? If so, you are too busy.

Take time to . . .
Learn the decisive, deliberate answer *no!*

Take time to . . .
Anticipate interruptions. They will come. Accept them as part
of God's training program.

Take time to . . .
"Commit your work to the Lord; then it will succeed." What
you honestly commit he takes. Whatever he touches he
changes.

Every day, Julie, you as a wife will be compelled to make
decisions: yes or no, this or that, now or later, red or blue, on
or off. Your choices will make some drastic differences in your
life—and in your marriage. But God can give you fresh
insights. His own word of promise is: "And your ears shall
hear a word behind you, saying, 'This is the way, walk in it,'
when you turn to the right or when you turn to the left"
(Isaiah 30:21, RSV).

God's Wedding Gift

Dear Julie,
The beautiful physical intimacy which you and Kent so eagerly anticipate on your wedding night is God's exquisite wedding gift to you—a gift wrapped in his own lavish love, colorfully ribboned with shining joy. His enclosure card is personally endorsed. It reads: "... *and behold, it was very good.*"

You understand, I'm sure, that the principle of your sexuality is overwhelmingly profound. In God's glorious creative plan it encompasses your total being: soul, spirit, body. It is a vital, vibrant expression of the self within. It pervades every particle of personality.

In the mysterious oneness of the sex act, the most intimate form of communication between a husband and wife, you and Kent will be saying to each other in a thousand secret ways ...

> I want you to know me, all of me, as I really am. I long to know you, all of you, as you really are. I am now and always a part of you. You are now and always a part of me. I give myself to you willingly, unreservedly, in full confidence of our love for each other.

Sex, *as God intended it*, Julie, is rich and refreshing, stimulating and rewarding. It is joyfully expectant. It is longing and belonging.

Sex, *as God intended it*, is total giving and accepting. It is trustful mutuality. It is a tremendous drive, a powerful source of unity, a reservoir of energy. It is the cooperative experience of meeting each other's stirring needs.

Sex, *as God intended it*, can be timid yet daring . . . awkward yet bewitching . . . quiet yet explosive . . . comforting yet susceptible to tears.

At times, Julie, it is space uncharted and time beyond scope. At other times it is like a worshipful cathedral.

At times it pulsates with magic and music. At other times it dances with laughter and mirth.

At times it races breathlessly up a windswept hill. At other times it is as quiet as dawn.

It can flame like a giant candelabra, or it can glisten like a mountain stream. It can banish loneliness and recapture wholeness. It can shatter restlessness and create incredible closeness.

Sex, *as God intended it*, is a language all its own, expressed in an environment of warmth and understanding. It is so much more than moments of passion—it is a promise of fidelity. It is so much more than a passing episode—it is the source of life. It is always love's servant, never its master. It is creative rather than destructive. It is venturous rather than violent. It delights rather than defrauds. It enriches, it elevates, it enraptures, it invigorates.

Sex, *as God intended it*, is a glorious celebration—a celebration of "the wonder of us" . . . the wonder of God! It is a dynamic gift to be reverently treasured and cherished.

Sex, *as God intended it*, partakes of heaven and intertwines with the marvelous creativity of God himself in the amazing miracle of birth and life. It is a lifelong partnership with him whose plan is wonderfully wise and good.

Let me say it again, Julie: *The intimacy of sex is God's exquisite wedding gift to you!*

The Bible makes it glowingly clear that God implanted the magnetic attraction between the sexes. The reasons are positive and explicit: The joyful expression of complete oneness. Mutual delight and release. Procreation.

It is always true that apart from the divine standards, sex can become grossly selfish, frustrating, even ugly and frightening. Today, when there is so much muddled thinking in our bewildered society, God's changeless imperatives have been rudely pushed aside—in fact, often flagrantly ignored. The result is the tragic impoverishment of thousands of lives. This reality we cannot camouflage.

But we need to get it straight that God is never out to cheat or frustrate us, nor does he fling his commands to thwart the consuming needs he himself created. With our sadly misguided concepts, we have shadowed the fact that his goal is our highest good in *every* specific—including sex. For every "thou shalt not" he graciously offers a counter "thou shalt have."

If you and Kent can genuinely *praise* God for the gift of your sexuality, you will begin to eliminate some of the crippling negatives you may have picked up at various times.

Anything that originates with God just has to be good!

Yes, Julie. *Yes!*

The Making of Music

Dear Julie,
Even though I've known you since you were in elementary school, I continue to discover new things about you in every letter you write.

In the middle of your letter this week you said, "Sometimes I wonder if I'll really be sleepable-with. I don't mean just while we're on our honeymoon, but *all* the time—year after year. Kent seems to think so—in fact, I'm pretty sure he's convinced! But I keep thinking . . . what if I should turn out to be a huge disappointment. I guess maybe I'm just scared. After all, I've never been a wife before."

When I shared your letter with Rollie, this was his only comment: "What a worry-wart!"

I wonder, Julie, do you happen to have any of your old assignment books from piano lesson days? Probably not. You were a little girl when I was your teacher, and many years have escaped since then. But you may remember that I always included a list of Helpful Hints with each new assignment: Count out loud! Watch your fingering! Observe the rests! Increase the tempo! Every week I'd write a new list, and the exclamation points were always intentional.

Once when I was writing your assignment, you surprised me by saying, "I really like the Helpful Hints. They help me remember." (I honestly think you were the only student who did!)

In a day or two, Julie, I'm going to compile another list— a list that has nothing whatever to do with piano lessons. However, I trust it will have the making of music in it for both of you.

I'm eager to share some guidelines, some basic reminders, relating very directly to the physical aspects of marriage. It is so important that you recognize your sexuality for what it is—a marvelous gift with breathtaking potential. As you rejoice in it, as you celebrate it, you will give unity and strength to your marriage.

So be happily optimistic as you share the guidelines together. I pray they may give you both some fresh, zestful insights. I'll get them off to you later this week.

Just one more thought: Frankly, I haven't a doubt in the world that you'll both stay "sleepable-with" for at least the next fifty years!

LOVING EACH OTHER AS WE DO
A Sacred Pledge

Loving each other as we do . . .

We joyfully acknowledge our sexuality as God's priceless gift—his unique and exquisite plan for our mutual fulfillment and total oneness.

It is our personal desire to bring honor to God, and wholeness to each other, in the physical expression of our intimate love.

We will accept openly our emotional and biological

differences, believing that God has fashioned each of us according to his wise and holy purpose.

We recognize that in each of us there are secret chambers difficult to penetrate: memories, inhibitions, impressions, childhood echoes . . . .

Loving each other as we do . . .

We will permit God to use our conflicts and damaged emotions as lessons in quiet growth. With loving patience, without ridicule or judgment, we will support each other in the gradual untangling of built-in defenses.

We will each focus on the other as a person, not as a pleasure—as a gift, not as a gimmick.

We will seek to please rather than to pressure, to delight rather than to demand, to give rather than to get.

Loving each other as we do . . .

We will regard our physical intimacy as the creative expression of a love already existing between us—never as a path leading to love.

We will share the humdrums as well as the highlights, the defeats as well as the victories, the awkward moments as well as the blissful.

We will not insist on perfection—rather we will anticipate growth. We will not compete for the mountaintop—rather we will climb the mountain together.

We will lift our hearts in a celebration of gratitude for God's marvelous love which made our love possible.

Loving each other as we do.

Ten Thousand Ways of Loving

Dear Julie,
Here it is—the list I promised you. I trust you will find the guidelines practical and helpful. More important, may they enrich your future years!

- *Expect to make adjustments.*

Your mutual goal is paramount—to bring to each other a deeply satisfying experience. This may take somewhat longer than you anticipate. In fact, let me put it more pointedly. In all probability it *will* take much longer than you anticipate.

"Rockets, rainbows, and rivers of joy," some of the marriage manuals say. Is that what you anticipate? Fine! Keep right on anticipating. At the same time, let your maturity come to the foreground. *Do* expect some trial and error.

- *Develop your own techniques.*

Sex at its best is total giving *to* and receiving *from* each other. Despite all you may have absorbed from the manuals with their expansive details, there is simply no "correct" method, no perfect Plan A or Plan B. No marriage counselor, however adequately trained, can fully explain it. No compatibility test, however exposing, can reveal the mystery of it. You are YOU, and this is beautiful, so do experiment *creatively*. Enjoy your own originality without laying down hard, fast rules—without frantically questioning, "What are we doing wrong?" Be free to tell each other what pleases you and what doesn't. Your goal is fulfillment without emotional damage.

• *Don't be defeated by irritations.*

Nagging worries about your job or family or finances can so easily deplete your energies. You won't always feel the same intense need at the same time. You may, in fact, be puzzled, even hurt, by unpredictable differences in tempo, in urgency and desire. But this is a fact to be accepted, not a resentment to be suppressed.

Be prepared, too, for some utterly ridiculous moments—moments eased only by good humor. There will be times when nothing will help more than spontaneous laughter.

• *Sort out the musty memories.*

Old and weary memories have a subtle way of trudging down familiar corridors. They tap at doors and windows with wooden canes. *"Hey,"* they whisper, *"make room for us!"* Buried secrets, hidden guilts, childhood wounds—how unexpectedly they surface!

Is there a quiet way of release? Can you be free from disturbing memories? Yes, Julie, to a great extent you can. How? Simply by sharing your fears and needs with each other openly and frankly.

The sharing might go something like this, Julie . . . .

"Once a kid in our block showed me some horrible pictures, and I dreamed about them at night. I thought, *I never want to sleep with anybody but me.*"

"Do you think your parents enjoyed sex? Did they ever talk to you about it? Did you think it was something repulsive?"

"Do men really think about sex all the time? Do you? Do you sometimes think about the dates you used to have?"

"When I was little, I pretended to nurse my doll one day. A neighbor saw me and called my mother, but I couldn't understand why. I just concluded that the lady never fed her babies."

"My college roommate told me her boyfriend possessed her, but I don't think anyone worth possessing is ever quite possessed—do you know what I mean?"

- *Never settle for a bargain-basement marriage.*

Several weeks ago, I overheard a short but pointed conversation between two male executives:

"Well, George, it really paid off last night. I must have done everything right."

"Great, Jim! Was it worth the new coat you bought her?"

"Sure thing." *(Pensive pause.)* "Wonder what it will take next time? Some marriage we've got!" *(Raucous laughter.)*

A cunning, conniving wife—or a manipulating husband— had made a bargain: sex in exchange for a new coat. Result: a bargain-basement marriage.

This is subtle, sad, sick. This is destructive. Sexual love is not an earned accommodation. It is not a bribe. *Sexuality, shabbily treated, reaps a marriage basically cheated.*

"Do not cheat each other of normal sexual intercourse . . ." the Bible clearly states (I Corinthians 7:5, Phillips). Reach out in loving availability to each other. As you do, a shining truth will continue to unfold: "It is [indeed] more blessed to give than to receive."

● *Recognize your differences.*

In the area of sex a husband is more inclined to think *now,* while a wife thinks *how? I want you,* a husband reveals. *Please need me,* a wife conveys. *Show me,* a husband asserts. *Let me tell you,* a wife responds.

It is vitally essential that you learn to accept your differences with growing maturity if you are to develop a healthy balance. Again the key word is patience.

● *Let love be your aim.*

As vitally important as sex is, it is not the answer to all marital happiness. It is a part of life, a part of the total package, but sex alone is never an adequate cohesive for a successful, satisfying marriage. It will not curb selfishness or dissolve jealousy or banish bitterness.

I ached for the young wife who sat in our living room one day. This was her pathetic story: "We read, studied, and pored over every manual we could find. Our sex life was, in all honesty, full of zip and zang. Yet, here we are—unbelievably discontent and desperate. *We just don't know how to love.*"

Love says, "I have an overwhelming desire for your highest good. I want above all else to have a share in the beautiful plan that God has for your life." Let love be your aim!

● *Let gratitude be your attitude.*

As you express gratitude to God and to each other for the love he has given, you will make an exhilarating discovery:

Your relationship will be continually enhanced.

There is a reason for this: Gratitude is always positive. It intensifies; it liberates and releases. Above all, it effectively unites your love with the creative love of God.

• *Learn ten thousand ways of loving.*

In all the years of my childhood, I doubt that we ever lived in a single parsonage where the sweet fragrance of roses didn't permeate the air. Roses were definitely a part of our family heritage, and I've never forgotten the summer ritual that made every breakfast a special event.

Every morning dad would come in from the yard with a freshly plucked rosebud—his personal token of love. Usually I'd be setting the table. I'd always feel a bit quivery inside when dad made his presentation to mother. With his own special brand of tenderness he'd say, "Here it is, sweetheart, your morning tribute."

One morning, while sunbeams played leapfrog on the kitchen wall, mother suddenly stopped stirring the oatmeal. She dropped her spoon. She threw her arms around dad and said, "Oh, honey, there are ten thousand ways of loving and you know them all!"

That's the story of, that's the glory of love! Gentle words, thoughtful courtesies, an out-of-the-blue surprise, a kiss on the nose, a love song . . . tiny things, tender things, day after day.

Julie, a love that is kindled in the kitchen is bound to be at its best in the bedroom.

I hope you and Kent will both learn ten thousand ways of loving—and always one more.

Learn to Be Happy with More

Dear Julie,

"For better or for worse" may often include "for more or for less"—especially when it concerns your bank account.

I had to learn the hard way.

In our early married days our apartment was located within walking distance of church, school, and town. We didn't have a car then, but it didn't matter much. It took me about ten minutes to walk to the center of town where I could gaze wistfully and longingly at all the dress shops with their fashionable window displays. I decided I needed the exercise—frequently.

One day, in the window of one of the most elite shops, I discovered a dream-dress that positively had my name on it. Everything about it was perfect: color, size, design—*everything*. I could tell it was right even before trying it on. Some things you just *know*.

Julie, I had never in my life opened a charge account. I was reasonably convinced, however, that it was a simple, painless procedure. You probably signed your name on a few blank lines, you gave several impressive references, and you walked out with the dress. After all, I reasoned, I was married now, and every wife should experience the elementary exercise of opening a charge account. It was a matter of responsibility!

The store manager happened to be a member of our church. She immediately recognized me, so there was no problem whatever. She was kind, solicitous, and very complimentary. It all turned out beautifully—exactly as I had anticipated. The dress fit perfectly! Signing my name came easily—it was fun to write *Mrs.*–and the box was light enough to carry away with a song.

But that night after I modeled the dress (Rollie liked it!), we had a long, detailed discussion about budgeting. The thrust of our discussion was: I wasn't working. Rollie was working. But he was going to school, too. As it happened, the dress was three times more expensive than our clothes budget allowed—with or without a charge account. I sat there just sorting mixed emotions during our lengthy conversation. Julie, it was such a *beautiful* dress!

Rollie didn't insist that I return the dress. He simply asked, with a little bit of a smile, "Do you really think you'd enjoy wearing it?" So what would you have done, Julie? Probably exactly what I did. The next day I walked back to the shop (slowly) with the box under my arm.

Well, we've come a long way since then. But I still think I've never seen a prettier dress in all my life than the one I reluctantly returned that long-ago day!

Surveys make it glaringly clear that couples and families are overwhelmed by the confusion of galloping inflation. To cut costs and make ends meet is an endless battle for all of us.

Julie, I personally believe that the one and only way to deal with the compounded problems of inflationary pressure is to make God our partner in our finances as well as in every other aspect of marriage. When he is our center of reference, materialistic goals are bound to become less consuming. Sure, problems still exist—we're faced with a constant barrage of them—but we have the spiritual insight to cope. That's the big difference.

Does it disturb you when I say that you and Kent will never have any money of your own? Rollie and I won't either. You see, life is a trust from God, and *all* that we have is his. Think about it a minute: What do any of us have that he didn't first give? Really, nothing.

What are some of the money traps we fall into so blindly?

1. *Keeping up with the Joneses.* Many couples simply can't handle prosperity—especially the prosperity of the couple next door. To try to keep up with the Joneses is both foolish and futile. Just suppose we finally make it. Around the corner live the Smiths. So it starts again—the competition.

2. *Poor management of funds.* Installment buying and personal loans can get out of hand quickly if we let impulse and emotion rule us. Wise budgeting is a must for economic security. It allows for daily expenditures. It allows for systematic giving and saving, for transportation, for insurance, for unforeseen emergencies. Budgeting also includes long-range planning. It includes paying off loans as quickly as possible and keeping accurate records for income taxes.

Money management is no easy thing. It involves restraint, discipline, control. It means commitment. It requires the ability to face responsibilities. I agree with the experts who say that money management is basically self-management. We tell much about ourselves by the way we handle money.

3. *The "my money" syndrome.* There are still husbands and

wives who have no idea how much money their mates earn. Vaguely, perhaps, but not totally. One wife confided that her husband had gotten three raises without her knowledge. She said, "I only know now because my husband's partner mentioned it inadvertently one day."

Another wife said, "I never tell my husband what I pay for things. If an item costs ten dollars, I tell him I paid five for it. He doesn't tell me how he spends money—so why should I tell him?"

Countless money quarrels result simply because mates think *me* instead of *we*. Mutual trust is shattered. One wife's caustic comment was, "We'll never be married financially."

Years ago Rollie and I "agreed to agree" on the distribution of funds. I don't check with Rollie every time I buy clothes or gifts or household items. When one of us comes home with something new, we don't say, "Now before we eat dinner I better explain that I paid exactly $3.79 for this." It just isn't that big a deal. We both know our budget—and we try to stay within it. The only time I say excitedly "How much do you think I paid for *this?*" is when I find some terrific bargain.

Charge accounts? Yes! But we set limitations. When large items are involved—like furniture and appliances and cars—we look, we consider, we decide together. We just don't purposely hide expenditures—that's the principle. The key word is honesty.

At our house Rollie keeps the financial records—by mutual agreement. He is decidedly more adept in this area than I am. In hundreds of homes the wife is the head bookkeeper—more power to her. How fantastic to be so capable! *Who* takes the responsibility is not as important as *how* it is done.

4. *The "someday" syndrome. Someday*, when we've bought a

bigger home, when we've put in our swimming pool, when we've settled on a new boat, when we've taken our big trip, *someday* we'll give more—we really will. We'll even give ten percent of our income. But right now there are so many pressing things, and well—it would be such a struggle. We just really can't afford to tithe.

But when giving becomes primary, and getting becomes secondary, we begin to see things from God's point of view. A whole new world opens up to us. The promise of Jesus is direct: "For if you give, you will get! Your gift will return to you in full and overflowing measure, pressed down, shaken together to make room for more, and running over" (Luke 6:38, TLB).

That's the way it is with him: All his gifts are running over.

Now for a few general practicalities:

Determine your budget *together.* Agree on a percentage savings program. Distinguish between your wants and your needs. Give until it no longer hurts. Why not start with ten percent?

Make friends with your piggy bank. For years we've had an almost sacred agreement about dimes. We don't spend them. Every summer our dimes make a sizable dent in our vacation expenses. Some couples save quarters—a marvelous idea.

Learn to be happy with—*more.* More music and laughter, more conversation, more friendships, more positive attitudes, more faith in God's lavish provision. All these gifts are free!

One thought about gratitude: You can never be thankful enough—but you can keep on trying!

It Takes a Lot of Little Things

Dear Julie,

Every happy marriage *must* have a lot of little things going for it if dynamic growth is the coveted goal. After thirty years of marriage, I have an overwhelming conviction that a raft of little things often keeps the one Big Thing from drowning in a swamp of mediocrity.

I like so much the way my friend Karen put it over the phone the other day: "We're determined to keep our marriage spicy—and we're discovering that it's the little things that add the spice!"

At first, Julie, it seems so easy—almost effortless much of the time. The little courtesies, the gentle glances, the unexpected surprises . . . they come so naturally. But to keep it from bogging down, to keep from gradually taking each other for granted—that's the real challenge.

I haven't a doubt in the world that after your wedding you and Kent will come up with some fantastic ideas—beautiful, original things that Rollie and I have missed completely. That's the way you are! But today, let me share just a few of the condiments that have added spice and zest to our marriage since the day we reverently said, "I do."

1. *Little surprises have flavored our joy.*

I've discovered that I still have a lot of little girl in me when it comes to surprises. The very word *surprise* worked its own magic during my childhood. I vividly remember my mother's mysterious way of making trivial things unbelievably exciting. She'd whisper, "I have a surprise for you!" and we were ready to take off. Mother even made creamed spinach sound exciting by calling it a surprise.

Early in our marriage we centered in on the Surprise Game. I don't know exactly how it started, but I *do* know we're both sweepstake winners.

I love Rollie's reaction when he finds a mystery package on his desk, especially after a long, tedious day. The gifts are never elaborate—a pair of sox, maybe, or a bottle of after-shave lotion. He's even excited when he finds a couple of candy bars tied with a huge red bow. Sort of ridiculous? Maybe. But spicy, too.

There was that day Rollie came home with an apple corer for me—*his* idea of a surprise. Somehow, he just couldn't fathom me going through life without an apple corer. Now an apple corer takes apples—and there I was with my shiny new gadget, and not an apple in the house. (It happens that way in marriage. One thing calls for another.)

Well, nothing else would do. Rollie dashed to the store and came back with the biggest, juiciest apples he could find. We had ourselves a coring party to surpass all parties. Then for a solid week we ate baked apples. Funny thing about that corer—it's still one of my favorite gifts.

I could go on telling you about the ridiculous, sweet, unusual, sentimental surprises we've brought home over the years, but you can work on your own surprises.

2. *Traditional days are memory-seasoners.*

If you ever want an unusual recipe for charcoal turkey, just talk to me. Our first Thanksgiving dinner was pretty catastrophic. But right in the middle of company dinner, somebody at the table (I don't remember who) hit on the idea of thanking God for the "charcoal turkeys" in our lives: the difficult things, the seeming disasters, that God had actually used for our highest good. As we shared together that day, an aura of gratitude surrounded the table. It was indeed a therapeutic hour. Every year since, we've taken time on Thanksgiving Day to thank God for the "charcoal turkeys" of the past year.

I've lost track of the times we've made our own valentines. Rollie is the artist (not me), so his valentines are much more professional. Usually I just write a note with hearts scattered all over the page. Does it take time? Well, yes—thoughtful things do take time. Marriage takes time!

3. *A Journal of Joy seasons our gratitude.*

After hearing a challenging sermon on gratitude one Sunday, we were shamefully aware of our careless response. Too often we take God's goodness for granted. As we drove home, an idea crystallized: We decided to keep an accurate two-month record of the day-by-day *unanticipated* joys God sent our way. I was elected Recording Secretary. Here's a sample of an "ordinary" week:

> Beautiful, unexpected letter from Rainy. Her loving letter sings in our hearts. (Thank you, Lord.)

> Sheila left some fresh flowers at our door with a darling "Sheila-note." (Thank you, Lord.)

The dentist bill was less than we anticipated. (Amazing, Lord. Thank you.)

You blessed us so much as we read from Hosea today. (Thank you, Lord.)

Pinki brought me a delicate butterfly necklace—a reminder of the cover of my first book. (Thank you, Lord.)

Julie, the experiment was transforming! We learned some valuable lessons: God is infinitely aware of little things, he so often blesses us through others, and an attitude of gratitude dispels doubt and increases our faith. A thankful heart is a peaceful heart.

4. *Renewed goals flavor all of life.*
Years ago we adopted a three-step plan for the first day of each new year:

- From our reading, we choose three Bible promises. We personally claim them for the new year, asking God to fulfill them in *his* way. We put no time limit on him, nor do we dictate the terms. We simply accept his Word. We are promise-oriented.
- We write down three personal goals for our individual lives. We share them, pledging prayerful support to each other in our endeavor to achieve. We are goal-oriented.
- We commit the year totally to God, always expecting much from him. We are God-oriented.

We have followed this plan through the years of our marriage. The result? He continues to surprise us with joy. Not happiness always, but joy. Happiness depends upon circumstances. Joy depends upon our relationship with him.

Julie, there are so many more things I could share with you, but I'm writing today to stimulate *your* thinking, not to suggest that you do it our way. Each marriage is beautifully unique—as yours will be. God isn't out for carbons.

Thousands of couples enhance their marriages in mature and fulfilling ways.

Lynn and Bill made every piece of furniture in their charming, love-filled apartment.

Bonnie is working to help Greg finish medical school. But they enjoy nothing more than an evening of relaxation before an open fire—listening to their superb collection of classical albums on their highly sophisticated stereo sound system.

Virgene and Chuck make miracles happen in their yard of blossom and beauty.

Vicki and Rick sing out their love to hundreds.

Wendy and Bob enjoy elegant candlelight entertaining.

But not all couples enjoy everything. A few husbands get nervous eating by candlelight. Some wives could do without scuba diving forever.

The essential thing is that you share *your* needs, *your* interests, *your* life-style with each other. Find your own spice. Keep it spicy *your* way—*but keep it spicy.*

Julie, it will never "just happen." It takes all of both of you. It takes determination. It takes imagination. It takes work.

But the One who sees the tiny sparrow fall is bigger than both of you. If you let him, he'll work *with* you.

He knows all about spice!

Keep It Klean and Kozy

Dear Julie,

However you feel about cooking (and I hope you feel good about it), your kitchen ought to be a happy room—not only for you but for everybody who walks through the door.

Let it wake you up in the morning with its shine and gleam! Really, it's a shame to have a groggy kitchen. There's nothing more unpleasant than getting up to a sinkful of messy, sticky dishes—it's enough to take the zip out of any morning. So even if you're always dashing off somewhere, do try to keep your kitchen from moaning, at least most of the time.

Is cooking boring? Well, it *can* be—if you settle for ruts! In our fast-moving society where we're used to change, almost anything gets boring after awhile. Even a cruise in the Caribbean every other week might bore us if we didn't spice it up with some variation. But cooking can be beautifully creative. It doesn't have to be all frustration.

Before too many months, Julie, you'll be into it. You'll be preheating your oven and greasing casseroles. You'll be "stirring constantly until smooth and thickened." You'll be baking "until hot and bubbly in the center."

If you've been steeped in some misconceptions, if some of your friends make a big weighty problem out of cooking, the whole thing probably looms like a monstrous drudgery.

It *is* a sizable task to manage a kitchen efficiently—don't let anybody tell you it isn't. It takes ingenuity to shop wisely and economically. It takes energy and forethought to plan nutritious, attractive meals.

But don't give up, Julie! Join the winners who practice and prove they can do it. Don't feel you have to make a big production out of every meal. Just let your meals be in tune with your natural bent for doing things. Your personality can permeate your cooking, too. Where do you ever find two wives who cook exactly alike? Let your creative planning express *you!*

Now for a few fun-thoughts from the word *kitchen:*

Keep it "Klean and Kozy"! We used to have a plaque in the kitchen of one of our old parsonages which absolutely fascinated me. It read: "Keep Your Kitchen Klean and Kozy." I couldn't understand why anyone would buy a plaque with misspelled words! But the advice evidently got through. I've never forgotten that plaque.

Imagination! Wake up, dress up, and beef up your ho-hum meals. Experiment with spices. Set a bright and sparkly table, too. Meals should be more than just food. Joy and laughter and communication ought to be part of every mealtime.

Tips! Get all you can from magazines and recipe books: short-cuts, wise buys, planned-overs, go-together dishes, more-value-for-less-money, start-to-finish ideas.

Care—tender and loving! Maybe you just can't *stand* liver and onions. Maybe Kent just *loves* liver and onions. Every once in awhile (without a word of complaint) fix liver and onions—with tender loving care.

Could be you just love pecan pie, and Kent does, too. One problem: calories! Kent doesn't have to watch them—but you? Well, that's another story. Occasionally, though (while you pray to resist temptation), bake a pecan pie—with tender loving care. There are numerous ways to say *I love you* in the kitchen.

Help, Lord! Have you ever noticed how the shortest prayers in the Bible got the biggest answers? I honestly think my mother prayed about every cake she ever baked. I know she prayed about dinner guests and menus and grocery shopping. She said one day, "After all, Jesus broiled fish over hot coals—of course he wants to guide me in the kitchen." It really is amazing how much more smoothly things go when we consult him about everything.

Enjoy! Easy-does-it isn't always so easy. At times you'll even suffer a mite of martyrdom as you stand over the stove. However, you really can learn to enjoy cooking if you flaunt a positive attitude. Develop your own specialties. Learn to do a few things with exceptional finesse. Sing while you saute!

Never give up! I like the plaque I saw in a downtown office: "Babe Ruth struck out 1,330 times." So no matter how frustrated you may feel at times, there's always another chance at a recipe!

One last fun-thought, Julie. If every now and then Kent wants to turn out a fluffy omelette, great! Let him take over while you read a good book.

Once in a While

Dear Julie,

On one clear, bird-singing Sunday of my twelfth year, I didn't want to go to church. That was all there was to it. I hadn't "backslidden," I wasn't coddling a pent-up rebellion, nor was I exhibiting a sudden streak of independence. I just didn't want to go to church.

The warm sun streaming through the windows added a quiet charm to our old house. I pictured a simple, leisurely day away from school and church and have-to things. I could sing my heart out at home if I wanted to—and if I didn't want to, I was sure God would keep right on loving me.

But how to broach the subject, how to explain my childish longing and be understood—that was the turmoil spinning inside me. After all, preachers' kids *always* went to church—just as regularly as they went to school. More regularly, in fact. At school you at least had vacations!

As I stood in the warm kitchen watching mother peel potatoes to add to the roast, thoughts kept tumbling. My secret longing persisted. Finally I just blurted it all out—how I wanted to stay home, how I didn't think God would mind a single bit.

Mother kept right on peeling potatoes. Not once did she interrupt me. Not a word about how I was disappointing her. She listened attentively, quietly, and somehow I sensed that she understood. When the last potato was peeled, she wiped her hands on her blue apron. Then very gently she put her arms around me.

"Honey," she said calmly, "you know we can't always do what we feel like doing. Nobody can. We would hurt ourselves and lots of other people, too . . . ."

Well, that settled it, I thought. I knew what was coming. Of course I'd have to go to church. It was silly even to talk about it.

Then suddenly I heard, "But once in a while we can! Once in a while we need a change. Once in a while we can do what we want to do—just because we want to. It's all right—you may stay home this morning."

I'll never forget that special Sunday and my peaceful sense of aloneness. Mother came home after Sunday school. When she asked how it felt to stay home alone, I couldn't explain my exhilaration—but I think she knew. We talked and laughed—and God was right there.

Julie, the memory of that day is still fresh and vivid. I've thought of it hundreds of times. Our marriage has been enhanced by it. Not because I stayed home from church, but because I learned a profound principle: *Once in a while we can!*

Once in a while we can get away from alarm clocks, phones, scouring pads, peanut butter jars, and milk cartons . . . away from the tempestuous, competitive workaday world in which we struggle to survive, a world which threatens and grabs and pushes and clobbers.

Once in a while we can find a quiet spot—a cabin or a

camper or a desert motel—away from nerve-shattering pressures and family and friends. Every now and then we need to reevaluate our marriage and rediscover the safe harbor of each other's arms. Battered emotions must be released. We need to step out of our ruts and moods and neuroticism. We need to recapture the magic again!

Once in a while as husband and wife we even need to be away from each other! Too often we lose the capacity for personal enjoyment. We need time to play alone, to pursue individual interests, to enroll in a class or join a club. We need to express our own God-given creativity. Togetherness becomes stronger when we're proud of our mate's personal achievements, when we can share our own talents.

Once in a while we need to walk alone, think alone, meditate alone. We need solitude and silence. God wants to hear our own private secrets. He alone can fully satisfy the deep longings of our souls. We are unique in his sight—we are not an echo of our mate. Our strengths, our skills, our abilities are wonderfully, blessedly *ours*.

Once in a while we need the luxury of a day or an evening we can call our own. Fishing . . . sailing . . . shopping . . . painting . . . driving . . . *enjoying*—without qualms, without guilt.

Once in a while it's good to get away! To forget? No, to fortify. To spend money foolishly? No, to invest wisely our lavish wealth.

Once in a while we can.

Who But You?

Dear Julie,

There are thousands of men in the world. Men come in assorted shapes and sizes, tall and short, big and small, wide and lean. There are politicians, salesmen, production managers, bankers, teachers and preachers.

But Kent isn't just any man—one out of the kit. He's *your* man, totally, exclusively—and no one will ever know him or love him as you do.

Who but you will know . . .

The heavy sound of his step at the end of the weary day . . . the shrug of his shoulders when he's utterly defenseless . . . the disjointed way he slumps in his comfortable chair, part of him on, part of him off . . . the way he always leaves his coffee mug on the floor next to his chair.

Who but you will know . . .

The feel of his strong shoulder when you're achingly weary . . . the way he tosses his pillow on the floor after he kisses you good-night . . . the way he reaches for your hand in the quiet darkness.

Who but you will know . . .

The cheerful sound of his whistle in the shower . . .

the sweet tang of his shaving lotion . . . the comical, awkward way he helps make the bed.

Who but you will know . . .

How he scowls when he's hungry . . . how he loves your breaded pork chops . . . how he can always eat one more scoop of ice cream . . . how he puts sugar on his tomatoes and salt on his grapefruit.

Who but you will know . . .

How he *knows* he's right even when he *knows* he's wrong . . . how failure taunts him . . . how his boss irritates him . . . how he clenches his fists when everything seems to blow up in his face.

Who but you will know . . .

His high moral courage . . . his refusal to fritter away life . . . the spiritual twinkle in his eye.

Who but you will know . . .

How restless he gets just before a vacation . . . how he says, "Someday we'll go to Switzerland," and you think—*Who knows? Maybe someday we will.*

Who but you will know . . .

How your heart explodes when he holds you close and says ever so gently, "Are you really for real?"

Julie, there are thousands of men in the world. Men come in assorted shapes and sizes. But Kent isn't just any man. He's *your* man—totally, exclusively—and no one will ever know him or love him as you do . . . except God! Be thankful for him, Julie. Kent is God's gift to you.

You are God's gift to each other.